Perioperative care of the child

By

Samantha Heath

Quay
Books

Quay Books, Division of Mark Allen Publishing Limited,
Jesses Farm, Snow Hill, Salisbury, Wiltshire, SP3 5HN

Mark Allen Publishing Ltd, 1998
ISBN 1–85642–147 3

British Library Cataloguing-in-Publication Data
A catalogue record for this book is available from the British Library

Printed in Great Britain by Redwood Books, Trowbridge, Wilts

Contents

Acknowledgements

The author would like to thank Rob Russell for agreeing to undertake production of the illustration within this book. My family, friends and colleagues who have been so supportive during its writing and who have read and re-read drafts during the course of this project. My husband Andrew who has, as always, been encouraging and patient especially during the times of my greatest frustration.

1

The nature of surgery and concerns for children

Key issues and concepts

* Technological advances in children's surgery and anaesthesia

* Changes in attitudes and approaches to nursing children

* Piaget's (1953) theory of cognitive development

* The child's concept of illness

Historical perspectives

The recognition of children's surgery and anaesthesia as specialist fields in both medicine and nursing has developed dramatically during the course of the twentieth century. All three specialist areas have, for the most part, developed simultaneously which is of little surprise given their relative interdependence today. However, history reveals that this was not always the case and for many years, children had surgery without anaesthetic on the basis that they were unable to appreciate pain and therefore, their suffering was minimal. As such, the first anaesthetic to be administered to a child did not take place until 1842 (Burns, 1997). Following this success, subsequent **technological advances** in anaesthesiology came as a result of the direct involvement of children. This was primarily because of their relatively good health in comparison to adults of the time (Burns, 1997). However, it has only been since the early part of this century that anaesthesia for children has been viewed as a speciality in its own right.

Children's surgery is also a recent addition to the many sub-specialities of children's health care. Modern pioneers include Denis-Brown, a British paediatric surgeon, and Ladd, an American. Denis-Brown is perhaps most famous for his addition to knowledge about the differences between child and adult anatomy and physiology and the development of surgical procedures for example, the removal of tonsils and the repair of cleft palates (Noble *et al*, 1997). Ladd's contribution to this speciality is best remembered because of his involvement with children injured in the explosion of an ammunition factory during World War 1. As a result, Ladd was able to make a series of recommendations for the care of children having surgery that are still just as relevant today. These include:

- proper diagnosis
- careful anaesthesia
- supportive perioperative care for the child.

(Burns, 1997; Noble *et al*, 1997)

Children's Nursing

Children's nursing has also seen some remarkable **changes in both attitudes and approaches**, particularly in the last forty years. The most fundamental of these changes is seen in the way in which families are now involved in caring for their children in partnership with health care professionals. This and other issues surrounding the admission of children to hospital, for example the need for specialist nurses and the environment in which children in hospital are cared for, have been debated since the 1950s when Bowlby and Robertson first demonstrated the enormity of the impact which separation from a primary care-giver could have on a child both in the short and long-term. Subsequently, further research, as well as government and independently commissioned reports have contributed to the extensive knowledge base concerning the need for specialist nursing intervention when children are, or are likely to be admitted to hospital. Now, it is possible to suggest that most children who are hospitalised will probably receive some kind of preparation either as part of a planned hospital based programme or as part of a collaborative venture between community health care professionals and school teaching staff. It is these trends in approaches to children's surgical care, which provide the basis for some of the current challenges for nurses and allied health care professionals. In addition, the changing technological, political and economic environment within the National Health Service contribute to the way children's health care services are delivered. Decreased admission periods for children requiring surgery and an increase in the need for day surgery, has ensured that nursing strategies for preparing children and their families for hospital are clearly identified (Nash and O'Malley, 1997).

Preparing children and their families for a period of hospitalisation has many purposes. Current evidence suggests that preparation can mitigate against the stress of hospitalisation for both the child and family (Ellerton and Merriam, 1996); reduce the fear and anxiety provoked by a strange and unfamiliar environment (Ziegler and Prior, 1997); it can improve post-operative recovery and decrease the long-term psychological problems encountered by some children (LaMontagne *et al*, 1996); and most simply, can offer reassurance and increase understanding of the need for hospital admission for all family members (Eiser, 1991; Ellerton and Merriam, 1996). However, it is also important to identify the way in which preparation for hospitalisation is organised must depend on the child and the family's understanding and assimilation of what they are being told. Equally, in order to deliver planned and purposeful care, the children's nurse must be able to appreciate how children's thinking develops in relation to common perceptions of illness and therefore, the purpose of hospitalisation. This must be done in conjunction with other aspects of development such as language and communication. A greater understanding of this development can be gained by examining Piaget's Framework of Cognitive Development (1953).

Cognitive development

Piaget (1953) suggested that children's thinking develops as a logical sequence of increasingly complex stages. He termed the four major stages in the process as:

- the sensorimotor stage (approximately 0–2 years)
- the pre-operational stage (approximately 2–7 years)
- the concrete operational stage (approximately 7–11 years)
- the formal operational stage (11 years and over).

The key events at each stage of development provide useful clues to the way in which children may perceive both illness and subsequent admission to hospital and, may also offer some indications about the type of methods which can be used to prepare children for such an event (see *Chapter 2*).

Sensorimotor stage

During the sensorimotor stage children begin to discover the relationship between their actions and the consequences and begin to develop what Piaget (1953) termed as, 'schemas' or mental ideas of objects and experiences. Importantly, Piaget (1953) explained that these schemas are developed through interaction between the environment and the child. Through this process of interaction, the child's attitude towards his environment changes during the first year and culminates in the development of 'object permanence'. That is to say that the child recognises that an object can exist even when it is out of sight. This is an important consideration for children's nurses since it means that the child is more likely to acknowledge the absence of their mother once this characteristic of thinking has been developed. Further, a concept of illness at this stage of development is not related to the cause and effect of disease, rather the illness is perceived in terms of separation from the parent. Bowlby (1953) suggested that the primary issues for the child separated from his/her parents are feelings of insecurity, abandonment and a loss of autonomy and independence. These feelings are often evident in the child's behaviour, for example crying, calling and searching for their parents. The child may also reject the attention of nurses who try to offer comfort. In this first stage of what is known as separation anxiety, the child may also show signs of distrust towards their parents when they return. If the period of separation from the parent is prolonged, the child begins to despair, feeling increasingly hopeless about finding the missing parent. This is apparent in the child's apathetic behaviour where comfort measures are instigated, for example thumb sucking. When separation is continued, children begin to repress feelings for their parents and regress to previous stages of development. Children become accepting of the care they receive and do not cry or protest when they are left. Although they may give the impression of having 'settled in' and begin to play with toys and respond to nursing staff, this is not the case. If a child reaches this level of distress at being separated from their parents, the psychological consequences can be long-term and far-reaching.

For younger children, the problems of separation are most evident in the relationship between child and parent especially in the bonding and attachment process that takes place during the early months after birth (Bee, 1995; Bowlby, 1953). Separation at this stage of development may cause disruption to the bonding process and impairment of the attachment between mother and child which risks the emotional and physical well-being of the child as well as the mother's ability to care for her child (Bee, 1995). Since children of this age do not have sufficient verbal skills to make their feelings explicit to people outside their immediate family, the importance of having a parent present where possible during a hospital stay becomes clear.

Pre-operational stage

Pre-operational thinking is characterised by a lack of reliable and logical thought processes. The child at this stage of cognitive development is unable to 'conserve' which put simply, means that the child finds it impossible to assimilate that the weight or volume of an object does not change even though its shape may do. Thus, it is possible to suggest that children who think within these parameters are easily influenced by their visual perception. This kind of thought process is in keeping with the way in which children understand illness (Muller *et al*, 1992). During this stage of cognitive development most children do not understand the concept of having internal organs and perceive that the body is made up of only that which can be seen (Eiser, 1991). Therefore, children in this stage of cognitive development will have greater concerns about equipment and instruments that can be observed rather than what may happen inside their bodies. In addition, children suppose that you are able to feel what they are feeling as result of their egocentric thought processes, and that you will understand the nature of their discomfort and so will do something about it.

Animism of thought is also present at this stage of cognitive development. This way of thinking contributes to the child's reasoning about the way in which disease is transmitted, for example by magical means. Furthermore, a significant number of children report that medical procedures are given as a punishment for being naughty or clumsy. It is probably as a result of this kind of primitive thinking that some children also fear mutilation as a consequence of being hospitalised (Eiser, 1991). However, older children within this group can suggest more empirical reasons about disease transmission and can understand the notion of contagion (Muller *et al*, 1992).

Concrete operational stage

Concrete operational thinkers are no longer reliant on the absolutes needed during the previous stage of development. As the thought process helps to develop the child's concept of the relationships between things eg. the child can express that something as subjective as pain can hurt a little or a lot and, can associate symptoms of their illness for example tummy ache and fever (Muller *et al*, 1992). This kind of association is also apparent in the way children are able to understand the relationship between illness and its treatment and that treatment is needed in order to get better. In spite of this apparent sophistication in their thinking, children at this stage of development still demonstrate an immature understanding of the relationship between illness and the internal functioning of their bodies. Consequently, children still believe that illness is largely caused by external factors but they are able to suggest that there may be some notion of contamination either by inhalation or ingestion or contact with others (Eiser, 1991; Muller *et al*, 1992).

Although more logical thought processes have replaced much of the egocentric behaviour identified in the previous stage of cognitive development, it is still important to note that children who think in this way cannot yet understand events and relationships they have not yet experienced. This has implications for the way in which children are prepared for hospital (see *Chapter 2*).

Formal operations

Thought processes at this stage are characterised by the ability to use and formulate hypotheses and to use abstract thought patterns without the need for concrete examples. There is also evidence to support that, with the development of more adult-like thinking, children are able to describe the cause and effect patterns of some illnesses (Muller *et al*, 1992). Here, infection and immunity are attributed as causative agents and the connection between such external causes and internal body failure is clear to the child. The child in this stage differs from children in the other stages of cognitive development as they now have an ability to hypothesise and reason individual alternatives. This means that the implications of disease processes on the child's future are well recognised and such insights enable this group of children to understand that the course of getting better may not always be very pleasant (Eiser, 1991; Muller, 1992).

Summary

Understanding the way in which children think about their world and, in particular, the ways they assimilate the nature of illness is vital for children's nurses. It means that explanations, activities and approaches to children of different cognitive abilities can be tailored to assist explanation of what is to come. Most importantly appreciation of the child's perspective can suggest how a child may respond to a new and potentially very frightening experience like hospitalisation. However, it should also be emphasised that not all children within each age group outlined here will respond in exactly the same way for a variety of reasons which will be discussed in *Chapter 2*.

As the rapid development of children's surgery, anaesthesia and nursing, as well as the technological, political and economic factors within the National Health Service continues to change, the response of nursing and allied health care professionals has been to adjust the delivery of children's services. This is especially evident in the reduced length of hospital admission for children and the increased level of day care services now on offer. As a result, strategies aimed at preparing children and their families for a period of hospitalisation more than ever take account of the child and family's ability to understand the nature of illness and the proposed course of treatment.

References

Bowlby J, (1953) *Child Care and the Growth of Love*. Pelican, Harmondsworth

Burns LS, (1997) Advances in pediatric anesthesia, *Nurs Clin North Am* **32**(1): 45–69

Eiser C, (1991) It's OK having asthma... young children's beliefs about illness. In: Glasper A ed. *Child Care: Some Nursing Perspectives*. Wolfe, London

Ellerton ML, Merriam C (1996) Preparing children and families for day surgery. In: Smith JP ed. *Nursing Care of Children.* Blackwell Science, Oxford

LaMontagne LL, Hepworth JT, Johnson BD, Cohen F (1996) Children's pre-operative coping and its effects on post operative anxiety and return to normal activity. *Nursing Research* **45**(3): 141–7

Muller DJ, Harris PJ Wattley L, Taylor JD (1992) *Nursing Children Psychology, Research and Practice.* 2nd Edition Chapman and Hall, London

Nash PL, O'Malley M (1997) Streamlining the perioperative process. *Nurs Clin North Am* **32**(1): 141–51

Noble RR, Micheli MS, Hensley MA, McKay N (1997) Perioperative consideration for the pediatric, patient: a developmental approach. *Nurs Clin North Am* **32**(1): 1–15

Piaget J (1953) *The Origins of Intelligence in Children.* Routledge and Kegan Paul, London

RobertsonJ (1970) *Young Children in Hospital.* 2nd Edition Tavistock, London

Ziegler DB, Prior MM (1994) Preparation for surgery and adjustment to hospitalisation. *Nurs Clin North Am* **29**(4): 655–69

Further Reading

The reading list that follows constitutes some of the most important documents that have helped to direct services for children in recent years. Fimiliarity with the recommendations they contain are essential for anyone considering working with children who are hospitalised.

Audit Commission (1990) *A Short Cut to Better Services: Day Surgery in England and Wales London.* HMSO, London

Audit Commission (1993) *Children First: A Study of Hospital Services.* HMSO, London

Department of Health (1991) *Welfare of Children and Young People in Hospital.* HMSO, London

DHSS (1976) *Fit for the Future. The Report of the Committee on Child Health Services The Court Report.* HMSO,London

Royal College of Surgeons (1985) *Commission on the Provision of Surgical Services: Guidelines for Day Care Surgery.* Royal College of Surgeons, London

2

Preparing children and their parents for hospitalisation

Key issues and concepts

• The child's developing concept of illness

• The child's preception of hospital

• The need to prepare children for a period of admission to hospital

• The philosophy of partnership with parents

The size of the problem

The National Association for the Welfare of Children in Hospital (1990) states that around 1 million children are admitted to hospital each year, and that a further 3 million children visit the Accident and Emergency Department for assessment and treatment or discharge. Of those children admitted to hospital, approximately half will be under the age of five years. However, the route of a child's admission to hospital is not exclusively via the emergency department, and many of those children for whom admission to a children's ward is a necessity, will be admitted for a planned (or elective) surgical intervention. For these children, it is almost always possible to instigate a programme of preparation for the experience in order to minimise the potential effects that a period of hospitalisation can cause.

The development of pre-operative preparation programmes for children has been an ongoing concern of children's nurses for some considerable time. The accumulative body of research generated over the last thirty years has contributed not only to knowledge about how such preparation should be conducted, but also to a greater understanding of the way that children perceive hospitals and the kind of issues which are worrying for children facing admission. A philosophy of family centred care adopted by many children's wards and the increased recognition of parents as partners in the care of their hospitalised children have further refined the direction of preparation activities.

Effects of hospitalisation

Admission to hospital is often cited as being one of the most stressful events in a child's life even when it is planned, although Douglas (1993) suggests that the experience is not always a negative one, particularly when the admission is a short, one-off event (Douglas, 1993; Zeigler and Prior, 1994; LaMontagne *et al,* 1996). In terms of change in children's post-admission behaviour, McClowry and McLoed (1990) agree as they were unable to identify any significant behavioural changes among the 50 school age participants in their study. However, Cross (1990) offers a different perspective, suggesting that a significant proportion of children experience short-term difficulties, for example nervousness about future separations and difficulties sleeping, when they return home from hospital. Certainly, responses like these could be considered typical, especially when they are compared with the key milestones of cognitive development and the child's concept of illness (see *Table 2.1*).

Table 2.1: The relationship between cognitive development, a concept of illness and the child's behaviour				
Age	Characteristics of thinking	Key milestones of cognitive development	Concepts of illness	Behaviour
0–2yrs	• Develop schema • Cause and effect • Interaction and reaction to the environment	• Develop object permanence	• No concept determined	• Respond to separation from primary care-giver
2–7yrs	• Easily influenced by visual perception • Unreliable and illogical	• Unable to conserve • Animism of thought • Influenced by visual preceptions • Egocentric	• The body is made up of what can be seen • Disease is transmitted by 'magical' means • Illness is a punishment • Some notion of contagion	• Fearful of mutilation • Respond to separation from primary care-givers • Regression of previously mastered skills • Guilty about being ill
7–11yrs	• Able to see relationship between things • Need concrete examples • Cannot think in abstracts	• Able to conserve • Concrete, here and now thinking	• Illness is caused by external factors • Understand that disease can be contagious by inhalation, ingestion or contact with others	• Fearful of mutilation • Respond to separation from primary care-givers • Worry about separation from school and peers • Become modest
11+yrs	• Do not need concrete examples • Can think about things that have not been experienced	• Able to hypothesise • Think in abstract terms	• Understand that disease can have causative agents	• Anxiety/ embarrassment • Anger/denial • Worry about effect on body image/sexuality • Worry about future implications

However, this type of picture does not wholly account for the many other factors that may contribute both to the child's perception of hospitalisation and the subsequent effects that this may cause. Indeed, Piaget (1953) recognised that the child's previous experience and interaction with the environment affected the way that children were able to assimilate new circumstances. Such a proposal is evident in the work of Sylva and Stein (1990) who identify that some groups of children are more at risk of being affected by hospitalisation than others. These writers identify children who are frequent hospital attenders or those who have lengthy admissions; chronically or critically ill children; anxious or nervous children; children who are alone in hospital and those who are not prepared for their hospital experience, as being the highest risk groups. Muller *et al* (1992) add that there may also be some correlation between other stressful life experiences prior to hospitalisation and the child's subsequent response.

The need to prepare children for hospitalisation

A way to tackle these issues and mitigate against the effects of hospitalisation for all groups of children has been the subject of numerous studies over the years (Hawthorn, 1974; Melamed and Siegel, 1975; Vinsintainer and Wolfer, 1975; Rodin, 1983; Eiser and Hanson, 1993; Ellerton and Meriam, 1996). Studies of this type include the work of Vinsintainer and Wolfer (1975) who identified that there were specific things that worry children about hospital admission. This study compared different kinds of preparation with children's reactions during hospitalisation. The groups identified were:

- physical harm, body injury, pain, mutilation and death
- separation from parents
- the strange and unknown and possibility of surprise
- the limits of acceptable behaviour
- the loss of control, independence and autonomy.

Later, Rodin (1983) concluded that the anxiety caused by invasive procedures could be reduced by preparation beforehand. In addition, she also suggested that there was some correlation between the anxiety levels of parents and anxiety levels of their children. Today, programmes of preparation build on this broad research base in conjunction with the principles of child development and so take account of the major features from each discipline. As a result, there are now a variety of methods available.

Sensorimotor stage (0–2 years)

The difficulties of preparing children adequately for hospitalisation are probably best illustrated within this group. As well as the fact that developmentally, children of this age are unable to perceive the nature of illness, other factors make the process of explanation more problematic due to their limited vocabulary and ability to express fears and concerns. Therefore, a great deal of skill, co-operation and partnership is required between play specialists, nursing staff and parents. This is because preparation for very young children takes place immediately before a procedure is carried out and has a different focus from preparation for older children.

The problems of separation and stranger anxiety are most visible. Therefore, the aim of preparation is to promote security and comfort by making sure that children are not additionally distressed by separation from their parents, however briefly. For very young children having surgery this may warrant careful preparation of their parents so that they can accompany the child throughout the event. Older children within the age group also require the close proximity of their parents, but may also benefit from the opportunity to use play as a medium to explore their new circumstances. Techniques that can be employed include using familiar dolls and teddies to demonstrate the fundamental aspects of going to theatre, and simple story-telling.

Pre-operational stage (2–7 years)

Children at this stage of development are very receptive to information. They enjoy learning and mastering new skills, which is almost always through play, either alone or with other children. Therefore, one of the most obvious ways to present information about hospital to children of this age is through play. Ziegler and Prior (1996) term this kind of preparation, 'therapeutic play', and suggest that it differs from normal play because it is outcome based and has purpose, whereas spontaneous play may not have. Purcell (1996) acknowledges that using play as the technique of choice for preparation among this group brings fun and normality to a very serious occupation. By handling real equipment, children can conceptualise the information they are being given which helps with mastery and subsequently, control of the situation. However, there is still a need for the information presented to be accurate. Children want to know about the procedural and sensory elements of being in hospital, for example, who they will meet, the equipment that will be used, and how it will feel, look and sound (Purcell, 1996; Ziegler and Prior, 1996). Verbal explanations that accompany this kind of play need to be clear, simple, realistic and honest and should avoid phrases that can be misinterpreted like 'cut off' or 'take out' and should be replaced with words like 'mend' or 'fix' (Purcell, 1996). Other means which can be used to facilitate a child's understanding about hospitalisation are story-telling and colouring books, which have the added advantage that they can be taken away by the child and referred to at a later date. However, it is to be noted that in some cases, parents do not share the professional view of the benefits of preparation and may perceive this as being a source of increased anxiety for children facing admission (Acharya, 1992).

The timing of preparation has been the subject of debate since the mid 1970s, although the consensus now seems to be that the younger the child, the shorter the interval between preparation and hospitalisation (Melamed *et al*, 1976; Adams *et al*, 1991; Ziegler and Prior, 1996). Usually, hospital-based schemes run about a week before planned admissions. Acharya

(1992) identifies that this is not always the best timing for younger children, but that other factors such as finance and time can preclude an extra visit to hospital for preparation.

Concrete operational stage (7–11 years)

The concerns of this group can be greatly influenced by social contact with their peers, friends and relatives. The type of information children may glean may not always be appropriate, or indeed correct. Therefore, one of the purposes of preparation for these children must be to correct any misconceptions. It is clear that children of this age group benefit from verbal explanations and that this can be in the form of 'peer modelling' as suggested by Bates and Broome (1986). Peer modelling is a way of learning by vicarious experience eg. watching a film that shows a child of the same sex being admitted to hospital for treatment without suffering any detrimental consequences. Purcell (1996) highlights that a similar effect can be achieved with the use of photographs and story-telling. Verbal explanations should be clear, honest, simple and unambiguous and language that may be construed by the child as threatening should be avoided.

Therapeutic play is also an important part of the preparation of this group. Therefore the role of the play specialist is integral. Often, dolls and teddies are beneficial in helping children to act out their fantasies and feelings where the use of the third person to 'talk' through their concerns is a useful coping and safety mechanism for the child. It is also possible to use this third person approach to help reduce some of the anxieties highlighted by Vinsintainer and Wolfer (1975). In particular, the fear of pain, mutilation and injury can be overcome by explaining how pain will be relieved or using dolls and teddies to explain the way the child's individual problem will be surgically corrected. Loss of autonomy and control can also be addressed through play, by encouraging children to choose toys, games, pictures and videos to bring with them on admission.

Formal operational stage (11+ years)

The principles of preparation for this age group, although similar to the previous groups in that explanation and understanding is essential, can be characterised by the depth of information required. Children of this age group often like to know more scientific and biological terminology in connection with their surgical procedure (Purcell 1996). However, this is entirely dependent on the individual and assessment of his or her informational needs. Similar techniques to those already cited can be adapted to convey information just as effectively. Particular issues in this age group are also comparable with Vinsintainer and Wolfer's (1975) categories of worrying aspects of hospitalisation. Changes in body image are especially important here, and explanation may be necessary about the kind of scar or surgical result that will be visible following the operation. Loss of autonomy and control are also sources of uneasiness. These issues can be tempered to some extent by encouraging the child's contribution and involvement in decision-making processes as far as possible.

Preparation for parents

The efforts which are made to ensure that children understand the nature and reasons for hospital admission, are obviously very important. Equally important, however, are the information needs of parents (Ellerton and Merriam, 1996). This is because hospitalisation of a child can cause alterations in the usual parenting role and changes to the parent-child relationship, with the result that parents are often highly anxious during admission (Purcell, 1996). The effects of parental anxiety are often seen in the child, who becomes increasingly anxious in response to the parents' demeanour. This notion of 'contagious anxiety' has been well documented in the literature of recent years (Rodin, 1983; Hayes and Knox, 1984; Ellerton and Merriam, 1996). Ellerton and Merriam (1996) suggest that there are two primary ways in which the effects of contagious anxiety can be minimised. The first of these is to assist parents in providing comfort and physical care for their children. Participating in aspects of care reduces feelings of guilt and helplessness. The second measure that can be used to reduce parental anxiety is through preparation prior to hospitalisation. Purcell (1996) contends that there are four categories of such informational need:

- knowledge about the procedures that the child has to undergo
- warning about changes in the child's appearance
- knowledge about possible changes in their child's behaviour
- knowing about the ward environment.

All parents will have different levels of need in each area depending upon factors such as previous hospital experiences, the child's condition and the method by which they have been admitted, anxiety levels and knowledge base. These must be assessed on an individual basis, taking into account the philosophy of partnership with parents.

Procedures

There are a number of published reports and studies available which demonstrate that the informational needs of parents are generally related to their child's condition, care and treatment (Lynn-McHale and Bellinger, 1988; Department of Health, 1991; Audit Commission, 1993; Long, 1997). It has been further identified that this information needs to be consistent, frequent and honest especially when the child is critically ill (Long, 1997). The purpose of clear and concise information is that it helps to reduce parental fear and anxiety and subsequently has a calming effect on children. For other practical reasons parents need to understand the procedures their child will undergo. Children are most likely to ask their parents about admission to hospital and treatment, and therefore the parents need to be in a position to give appropriate answers that are in keeping with both the nature of the procedure and likely experiences of their child. Parental understanding is also essential for consent to surgery (see *Chapter 3*).

Changes in the child's appearance

The nature of some kinds of surgery means that there will be a considerable change in the child's appearance. This can be an extremely frightening experience for parents who may feel helpless and overwhelmed. If dramatic change is anticipated, for example following some types of urological, bowel or cardiac surgery or where the child will return to the children's intensive therapy unit (ITU), parents can be prepared using similar principles to those identified earlier. Methods of particular value in preparing parents are using photographs or diagrams and, where possible, introducing other parents whose children have had similar procedures.

Behavioural changes

Surgery can be an enormously stressful experience for children especially when the procedure is a major one and involves a lengthy admission and the possibility of a period of intensive care. Parents need to know that as a response to their stress, children's behaviour can change. This may be demonstrated in angry outbursts, confusion and regression to previously mastered aspects of behaviour (Purcell, 1996). It is important for parents to be able to recognise that during such episodes it is reassuring for their child to have them close by, even though this can be very upsetting to watch.

The environment

Just as the ward environment can be frightening and unfamiliar for children, so parents can be worried by the prospect of admission. Previous hospital admissions, either personal or with other children, can contribute to the anxiety felt by parents. From a practical perspective parents wonder what to bring and what facilities will be available and it can be reassuring for parents to have information about these aspects prior to admission. This kind of orientation can help parents understand what to expect and can reduce the fear of the unknown.

Summary

Preparing children and their parents for hospital is an essential aspect of the perioperative care of the child. Nurses and allied health care professionals need to have an understanding of the way in which children view illness and hospitals, as well as how appropriate teaching methods can be used to meet the distinct needs of all groups of children and their parents. Children's nurses also need to appreciate how particular individuals may be more susceptible to the stresses of hospitalisation and therefore need to be able to use their caring skills as a means of alleviating the problems that have been identified. It is clear that by using these principles of preparation for children and their parents, the hospital experience can be incorporated into family life without causing undue additional stress and anxiety.

References

Acharya S (1992) Assessing the need for pre-admission visits. *Paediatr Nurse*. 4(9): 20–3

Adams J, Gill S, McDonald M (1991) Reducing fear in hospitals. *Nurs Times* **87**(1): 62–4

Audit Commission (1993) *Children First: A Study of Hospital Services*. HMSO, London

Bates TA, Broome M (1986) Preparation of children for hospitalisation and surgery: a review of the literature. *J Paediatr Nurs* **1**(4): 230–9

Cross C (1990) Home from hospital. *Nursery World* **90**(3228): 22–3

Department of Health (1991) *Welfare of Children and Young People in Hospital*. HMSO, London

Douglas J (1993) *Psychology and Nursing Children*. Macmillian, London

Eiser C, Hanson L (1991) Preparing children for hospital: a school based intervention. In: Glasper A ed. *Child Care: Some Nursing Persectives*. Wolfe, London

Ellerton M-L, Merriam C (1996) Preparing children and their families for day surgery. In: Smith JP ed. *Nursing Care of Children*. Blackwell, Oxford

Hawthorn P (1974) *Nurse — I Want My Mummy!* Royal College of Nursing, London

Hayes VE, Knox JE (1984) The experience of stress in parents of children hospitalized with long-term disabilities. *J Adv Nurs* **9**(4): 333–41

LaMontagne LL, Hepworth JT, Johnson BD, Cohen F (1996) Children's pre-operative coping and its effects on post operative anxiety and return to normal activity. *Nursing Research* **45**(3): 447–53

McClowry SG, Mcloed SM (1990) The psychological responses of school age children to hospitalization. *Children's Health Care* **19**(3): 155–60

Melamed BG, Meyer R, Gee C, Soule L (1976) The influence of time and type of preparation on children's adjustment to hospitalization. *J Paediatr Psychol* **1**: 31–7

Melamed BG, Siegal J (1975) Reduction of anxiety in children facing hospitalization and surgery by use of filmed modelling. *J Consulting and Clinical Psychcology* **43**(4): 511–21

Muller DJ, Harris PJ, Wattley L, Taylor JD (1992) *Nursing Children Psychology, Research and Practice*. 2nd Edition. Chapman and Hall, London

NAWCH (1990) Needs and services. Children in surgery. *Nursing Standard Special Supplement* **4**(24): 14

Piaget J (1953) *The Origins of Intelligence in Children*. Routledge and Kegan Paul, London

Purcell C (1996) Preparation of school-age children and their parents for intensive care following surgery. *Intens Care Crit Care Nurs* **12**(4): 218–25

Rodin J (1983) *Will This Hurt?* Royal College of Nursing, London

Sylva K, Stein A (1990) Effects of hospitalisation on young children. *Newsletter of Association for Child Psychology and Psychiatry* **12**: 3–9

Vinsintainer MA, Wolfer JA (1975) Psychological preparation for surgery pediatric paitents: the effect on children's and parents' stress responses and adjustment. *Pediatrics* **56**: 187–202

Ziegler DB, Prior MM (1994) Prepartion for surgery and adjustment to hospitalisation. *Nurs Clin North Am* **29**(4): 655–66

Further reading

The articles listed below offer excellent accounts of additional perspectives of the ways in which children understand their bodies, their health and illness. Both would be extremely useful when considering other children's nursing specialities besides surgery.

Gaudion C (1997) Children's knowledge of their internal anatomy. *Paediatr Nurs* **9**(5): 14–17

Rushforth H (1996) Nurses knowledge of how children view health and illness. *Paediatr Nurs* **8**(9): 23–7

3

Pre-operative care

Key issues and concepts

- Immediate pre-operative preparation

- Current debate in children's pre-operative care

- Children and consent

- Nursing responsibilities in pre-operative care

Pre-operative considerations

A major feature of pre-operative care is found in the attention dedicated to ensuring that wherever possible, children are appropriately psychologically prepared for a period of hospitalisation. Although pre-operative preparation can be planned for children needing elective surgery, the same is not always true for children requiring emergency treatment, and these children demand alternative forms of preparation at the time of admission (see *Chapter 7*). However, all children have unique psychological needs. Attention to these needs constitutes a considerable part of pre-operative nursing care. Therefore, it is essential that children's nurses understand the ways children develop a concept of illness, the effects of hospitalisation on different age groups and how these theoretical concepts are implemented into nursing practice in partnership with families.

Other considerations that are essential to the pre-operative nursing care of children are related to anatomy and physiology. Particular differences between the normal anatomy of a premature baby, a neonate, infant, child or adolescent need to be addressed in conjunction with the presenting problem requiring surgical intervention. Examples of these differences are found in body size, surface area, and structural variances in airway and circulatory anatomy. These aspects inform the process of planning and delivery of nursing care. Depending on the nature of the surgical procedure and the type of intervention required, delivery of that care may involve several groups of health care professionals. Each professional group has their own area of expertise and, when their contributions are viewed in collaboration with the other groups, they enhance the care delivered to the child and family. Co-ordinating the contributions of all the allied health care professionals is usually one of the significant pre-operative care roles adopted by nursing staff.

Co-ordinating pre-operative care needs to be planned purposefully. Davies and Klein (1994) suggest that this can be achieved using four aims of pre-operative evaluation. Activity is directed towards:

- optimising the health of the child before surgery
- reducing the child and family's anxiety through teaching and planning
- planning perioperative management
- assessing pre-/post-operative health care needs for discharge and follow-up.

Although the principles of surgical care are similar for any child, the kinds of specific activity involved in meeting each of the aims will vary according to whether admission is as an emergency or is for elective surgery either as a day case or in-patient. The special needs of children needing emergency or day care admission are discussed in *Chapters 6* and *7*. The needs of children and their families attending hospital for elective surgery follow.

Optimising the health of the child before surgery

Elective admission for surgery rarely warrants the extent of stabilisation procedures involved in an emergency admission. Therefore, the aim of care in an elective admission is to assess that the child's general health has remained good in the intervening time since surgery was planned. A variety of methods can be used to accomplish this task, but the first is usually by a process of non-invasive assessment techniques. Throughout this pre-operative assessment phase of admission, the nurse's responsibilities are clearly located in the development of a thorough and accurate assessment of the child and family, including the establishment of a trusting relationship. Such an assessment is normally carried out as part of the application of a particular model of nursing which is used to guide the delivery of nursing care through stages known as the nursing process: assessment, planning implementation and evaluation. Initial assessment is a key feature of nursing care since it will form the basis of future care options throughout the child's stay. The kind of information gathered refers to physical, psychological and social circumstances relevant to admission. This includes usual patterns of behaviour, levels of functioning and a detailed comparison of aspects of the child's life that have changed as a result of the underlying condition or hospitalisation. In addition, baseline information is gathered during assessment and this will be used during the post-operative period for example, pulse rate, breathing patterns, blood pressure and the kind of measures which the child finds comforting. (A sample assessment is provided in *Chapter 9*). The nurse's role will involve the co-ordination of other pre-operative assessments and investigations that need to be made.

Medical assessment is systemic and involves determining the child's suitability for anaesthesia and current condition both in relation to the underlying problem requiring surgical intervention and pre-existing disease. Other methods used for pre-operative assessment in elective admissions can include blood counts, coagulation studies and, where there may be evidence to support the presence of a major haemoglobinopathy, eg. sickle cell anaemia, testing for this will also be undertaken. Chest, other types of X-ray and some forms of scanning may also be used for the purposes of visualising the location of a tumour for example, or to determine the best kind of surgical intervention. However, there is some discussion at present about the relevance of undertaking some of the more routine measures of pre-operative assessment. Nash and O'Malley (1997) report that pre-operative chest X-rays rarely reveal any significant abnormalities that cannot be detected by history and examination of the child. The purposes of pre-operative urinalysis in children admitted for non-urological surgery has also been debated where minor abnormalities in the urine are unlikely to defer surgery. However, such issues are contentious and the reader is advised to check local policy.

Reducing anxiety

Reducing anxiety during admission for both the child and parents begins with appropriate pre-admission preparation and has been discussed at length in *Chapters 1* and *2*. For some children though, there will be the necessity to undergo procedures which were not initially anticipated. In cases like these, preparation can take place on the ward with the same effectiveness as that undertaken prior to admission. When necessary, methods chosen to supplement pre-admission preparation are tailored to the specific nature of the investigation and the child's developmental ability. In undertaking preparation in these circumstances, the greatest asset of the children's nurse is the parents. However, they too have a number of anxieties in the pre-operative period, although these can be addressed with considerate planning and forethought.

Examples of the ways in which parental needs can be met in practice are found in the work of Bradford and Singer (1991). These researchers were able to determine that when parents received detailed and structured information tailored to the family needs, it correlated with greater parental satisfaction during hospital admission. Greater satisfaction, it is deduced, may have been due to the more general availability of written literature and the less frequent incidence of conflicting verbal information about the child's condition. Blair (1995) highlights other issues that can be instrumental in reducing stress and anxiety among parents during admission. In her survey of parents and nurses, she identifies a large variety in facilities for personal needs and sleeping accommodation offered to parents of children in hospital. However, it is rightly asserted that the provision of a wide range of facilities within the vicinity of the ward can avoid the problems faced by parents who do not want to leave their child to go in search of these facilities elsewhere within the hospital complex (Blair, 1995). Such concerns were similarly reflected in the joint position expressed by the Caring for Children in the Health Services Group (1988) where recommendations for the provision of overnight accommodation were outlined (Thornes, 1988). Although these standards are widely acknowledged, there is still some way to go before such recommendations are uniformly implemented and the consequent benefits are given to parents accompanying their children during a period of admission.

Planning perioperative management

In the **immediate pre-operative phase of care**, nursing activity is directed towards maintaining the physical safety of the child. This is achieved by ongoing assessment and planning of individual aspects of care, and ensuring that this is documented and communicated to theatre staff. *Figure 3.1* illustrates a 'theatre checklist'. Such a document ensures that there is a quick and easy reference to essential information that may be required during the operative phase of admission. In most children's hospitals the theatre checklist is also designed to be as child centred as possible so that theatre staff are able to communicate with the child in ways that are familiar to them.

Figure 3.1: Sample Theatre Checklist (adapted from Smith, 1995)

Personal Information

Child's Name:		Hospital No:		Ward:
Likes to be called:		Consultant:		
Address:		Proposed Operation:		
		Allergies		

Pre-operative Physical Assessment

Pre-operative Observation: Temperature Pulse		Respiration	B/P	Cuff size Limb
Weight	Height	Urinalysis		Sickle Cell Result

Checklist

Identification bracelet checked		Y	N	
Consent form signed		Y	N	
Pre-medication given		Y	N	NA
Pre-cannulation cream applied Site:		Y	N	NA
Fasted Time of last drink Time of last food		Y	N	
Jewellery removed/made safe Site:		Y	N	NA
Make up/Nail varnish removed		Y	N	NA
Prosthesis/Contact lenses removed		Y	N	NA
Braces removed		Y	N	NA
Loose teeth/caps/crowns Site:		Y	N	NA

Equipment in situ pre-operatively

	Site:
	Site:
	Site:
	Site:
	Site:

Figure 3.1: continued		
Accompaningy Child to Theatre		
Case notes:	Y	N
X-Rays	Y	N
Toy/Comforter Describe	Y	N
Parent Explanation:	Y	N
Child's Individual Needs		
Special Instructions:	Preparation for high dependency following surgery:	
Child would like sutures/plaster etc. following surgery:	Special words used by the child:	
Other needs:		
Ward Nurse Signature:	Theatre Staff Signature:	
Date: Time:	Date: Time:	

Categories of information included are personal details; physical assessment; a safety checklist; notes about any devices which are in situ prior to surgical intervention; equipment accompanying the child to theatre, and special instructions about the child's individual needs. At first sight, the organisation of the theatre checklist is apparently a task centred and a ritualistic type of format. However, the reasoning underpinning its use are far from being either of these, and there is good evidence to support the inclusion of all the elements shown.

General anaesthesia and recovery from surgery means that the child may not always be able to communicate reliably or effectively with theatre staff. In addition, the child's age and developmental stage may also contribute to such circumstances. Therefore, personal details are included in this type of nursing record so that theatre staff are able to provide the right care for the right child and can document this in the right record. Physical assessment details include documentation of baseline observations so that comparisons can be made both during and after surgery (see *Chapter 4*). Weight and height are essential components of the record because these measurements provide information upon which drug dosages can be calculated. Allergies are also noted to avoid administration of potentially harmful drugs and to inform decisions made about the type of wound dressings that will be most appropriate for the child following surgical intervention.

The safety checklist is another source of pertinent information for the theatre staff. However, issues surrounding consent, fasting and parents in the anaesthetic room are at present the subject of particular debate and are discussed more extensively later in the chapter. The remaining aspects of the checklist are more easily dealt with. Pre-medication for elective surgery principally depends on the nature of the surgery. In minor elective surgery, pre-medication is not always given for the simple reason that pre-operative sedation can lengthen the time that it takes for the child to recover post-operatively. For major elective surgery, it can be given, but attempts are made to ensure that where possible this is given orally avoiding the intramuscular route. In both cases, pre-cannulation cream is applied where no intravenous cannula exists and it is clear that one will need to be inserted before the child is anaesthetised for the purposes of induction. This is applied to the backs of both the child's hands one hour before surgery is anticipated, according to the manufacturers guidelines. Use of this cream requires the co-operation of the child's parents, and they need to be asked to prevent their child from eating the cream because of its local anaesthetic effects. Parents also need to be told that the site of the application of the cream may demonstrate signs of erythema, oedema and blanching which are normal side-effects.

Jewellery is a hazard because it can catch in other theatre equipment and cause unnecessary personal injury to the child or theatre staff. Where possible it should be removed and stored for safekeeping by the family or by ward staff according to local policy for valuables. However, in some instances religious or cultural convention may dictate that the removal of particular pieces of jewellery is not appropriate. In such circumstances, accommodation of the child and family's wishes for the jewellery to remain in place is nearly always possible by taping over the object and making sure that theatre staff are aware of its presence. Liability for loss or damage to the item in such circumstances needs to be thoroughly explained to the family.

It is better to remove all make-up, but in cases where there is a particular reluctance to do this, it should be kept to an absolute minimum. In particular, lipstick and heavily applied foundation should be totally avoided because of the difficulties this causes for theatre staff in being able to observe any colour changes in the lips and circum-oral area indicative of poor oxygenation of the tissues. Nail varnish too, should be removed in all cases for similar reasons and so that nail beds can be observed for colour changes also associated with poor peripheral oxygenation. The presence and location of dental work and loose teeth must also be documented because of the risks of accidental removal during intubation in general anaesthesia and the risks this presents in the potential for such items to be inhaled.

Safety is again the primary concern when documenting any equipment such as intravenous infusions, catheters or cannulae, which are in situ prior to transfer to theatre. The site is noted on the theatre checklist to prevent accidental removal or injury to the child. It is also important to take associated documentation to theatre with the child for example, fluid balance charts, because theatre staff will need to know the type and volume of fluid infused, related output and cumulative fluid balance for the day of surgery. Other items accompanying the child to theatre are also itemised on the checklist to ensure that there is a record of their location during transfer. In particular, special words, comforters and other needs are clearly identified to assist theatre staff in continuing the individualised care started at admission.

The general principles of perioperative management then, are related to maintaining the safety of the child throughout the procedure, both in physical and psychological terms and can be achieved in many of the ways previously discussed. However, this does not mean that all aspects of care are widely accepted in spite of good evidence to suggest that they should be adopted. Of particular note are the debates surrounding pre-operative fasting and the relative merits of parents accompanying their children into the anaesthetic room. In addition, the issues surrounding children's consent to surgery provides some challenging debate for those working in this field.

Until recently, the purpose of **pre-operative fasting** has been commonly cited as reducing the risks of pulmonary aspiration of gastric fluid. Although evidence from historical and retrospective analysis of children's medical records in America reveals that the incidence of aspiration is around three times higher in children than adult surgical patients, the risk still remains as low as 1:46 000 (Burns, 1997). Perhaps more significant to the care of children requiring surgical intervention, is the categorisation of conditions and circumstances which increase that risk. Burns (1997) identifies the following factors:

- the time since the last meal
- mechanical or functional obstruction to digestion
- gastro-oesophageal junction dysfunction

- unco-ordinated swallowing and respiration
- level of consciousness/neurological damage
- physical injury.

For children requiring an elective surgical intervention, the most pressing issue is related to when the last meal was taken. Research by Schreiner (1994) has indicated that when standard fasting (8 hours) is compared with a drink of clear fluid (3ml/kg) 2–3 hours before surgery, there is no difference in either the residual volume of gastric contents or the pH between each sample. Physiological evidence also suggests that this should be so, since it is widely accepted that gastric emptying depends upon the type of content of the stomach (solid or liquid) and the composition of that content (protein, fat or sugar). Also, there is a greater risk of hypoglycaemia in children fasted for more than 6–8 hours as well as an increased risk of the development of dehydration and electrolyte imbalance (Bates, 1994). Therefore, Burns (1997) argues that the focus of care for the elective surgical patient should not be aimed at preventing a rare complication, rather that a 'safe' procedure should be drawn up. Bates (1994) offers a useful consideration of the way in which audit can be used to highlight such problems among the child population of surgical patients. His work in a day case unit allowed the instigation of individual fast times for children undergoing elective procedures. The results of his work demonstrate that far fewer children had to fast for several hours prior to their surgery without any commensurate increase in the incidence of pulmonary aspiration of gastric contents. However, making changes to established practice is not easily achieved, and it can take great effort and perseverance in order to accomplish even small modifications, especially where this calls for multi-disciplinary and multi-department co-operation. However, as a result of continued interest in the topic, guidelines produced generally recommend fasting times of the following order:

- food: 4–6 hours
- formula milk: 3–4 hours
- juice/breast milk: 2–3hours.

Parents in the anaesthetic room

Another example of changing practice is the increasing presence of parents in the anaesthetic room during the induction of children's anaesthesia. It is not a development that has always been widely welcomed and resistance is usually on the grounds that parents may interfere with the induction; that they may faint and become patients themselves, or that they would become too frightened and upset if something unexpected and untoward happened to their child. Although such comments are understandable, they are simply not adequate as reasons to prevent parents accompanying their children during the induction of anaesthesia. When parents are given the opportunity to receive appropriate preparation beforehand and support during the event, they are effective in reducing the fear and anxiety of their children and are a great asset in instigating calming and comforting measures. Where there is evidence to suggest that induction will be difficult because of underlying medical problems, parents are quite capable of understanding that their presence may not always be appropriate. However, the benefits of having a parent present at induction for the child include a reduction in the fear associated with a strange and frightening environment, and separation from their family at a time of great stress.

Consent to surgery

At the present time, the ability to give **consent** for an operation to take place is only possible when a person is over the age of sixteen. As such, most children will need to have consent given for them either by their parents or by the person who has 'parental responsibility'. Parental responsibility is held jointly by the child's mother and father if they were married at the time of the child's birth. When a child's mother and father are not married at the time of the birth, the mother automatically has parental responsibility. In cases like these, the father must apply for adoption of the child in order for him to acquire joint parental responsibility with the child's mother.

Consent is needed for all routine and non-routine procedures including photography, research and the release of medical records. Only in exceptional circumstances will consent not be sought from the people who have parental responsibility for the child. Such circumstances arise when the child needs emergency treatment because there is an immediate threat to life or when serious complications arise during surgery and the delay in seeking parental consent would threaten the life of the child.

Superficially then, giving consent for a child's surgery to take place seems straightforward. However, the issues are complicated by the fact that it is not simply consent to surgery that is asked for, but that informed consent is acquired. This means that the person who is giving their consent for the surgery to take place must understand the need for surgical intervention, the nature of the procedure and the likely outcomes and consequences of the surgery. One might suppose that the task of ensuring that parents give their informed consent for their child's surgery would be difficult enough, but the issues are further complicated by the notion that a 'mature' child can also give their consent to surgery. In practice this means that a child who is under the age of sixteen but has the ability to assimilate the implications of undertaking the proposed course of action or not can give their assent or decent to the procedure taking place (Children Act, 1989). The particular difficulties in this situation are observed when there is a dispute between the 'mature' child and their parents' wishes. Current debate on this issue questions how far it is possible or appropriate to allow 'mature' children to make such decisions for themselves, particularly when there is more than a measure of controversy about the exact nature of truly informed consent and what is understood may not always be wholly accurate. Other types of dispute surrounding informed consent usually occur between those with parental responsibility and the medical staff. Situations like these happen when the parents will not give their informed consent for a procedure to take place because of their personal beliefs. In such situations where a decision not to proceed with treatment would threaten the life of a child, a Court Order is obtained to allow medical staff to carry out the procedure.

Assessing health care needs

An assessment of health care needs should encompass the whole surgical experience for the child and family from admission to discharge and beyond. The function of such an assessment is to assist the planning and implementation of care measures which may not be revealed on assessment of the child and family alone, but that will be necessary as part of the recovery and rehabilitation process. The kinds of issues that are commonly highlighted are related to opportunities for teaching, liaison and health promotion. Examples of this type of planning are found in the pre-operative teaching of certain skills like walking with crutches so that the child feels more confident when they need to use these in the post-operative period; the demonstration of the use of patient controlled analgesia pumps, and preparation for changes in body image following surgery.

Parents also have learning needs especially where they have agreed to take responsibility for complex procedures and equipment when the child is discharged from hospital. An assessment of health care needs can assist in identifying the appropriate timing and planning for learning and teaching to take place in preparation for these events. Other advantages of the assessment of health care needs are the early development of liaison between ward staff, specialist nurses where appropriate, and community staff in preparation for discharge. Where health promotion needs are identified these can be addressed during admission or as part of the child's individual discharge plan.

Summary

The effort involved in thoroughly preparing the child and their family for admission to hospital for elective surgery is enormous, and is often conducted in circumstances where there is not as much time available as children's nurses would like. Therefore, it is important to understand the role of each aspect of care and its contribution to the whole experience of elective surgery both for the child and the family. For the children's nurse this means having an excellent understanding of the psychological aspects of child development and the ways in which such knowledge can be used effectively in pre-operative care. Here, nursing responsibilities are clear and are directed towards maintaining the physical and psychological safety of the child as well as communicating relevant care needs to other professionals involved with the child and family.

Much of the pre-operative care offered to children requiring surgery is based on sound rationales and knowledge although there are still areas in which there is room for improvement and collaboration. Such issues will no doubt continue to challenge nurses into the next century and hopefully improve the whole experience of surgery for the child.

References

Bates J (1994) Reducing fast times in paediatric day surgery. *Nurs Times* **90**(48): 38–9

Blair K (1995) Facilities for parents. *Paediatr Nurs* **7**(4): 18–21

Bradford R, Singer J (1991) Support and information for parents. *Paediatr Nurs* May:18–20

Burns L (1997) Advances in pediatric anaesthesia. *Nurs Clin North Am* **32**(1): 45–69

Davis JL, Klein RW (1994) Perioperative care of the pediatric trauma patient. *AORN Journal* **60**(4): 559, 561, 563–5

Nash PL, O'Malley M (1997) Streamlining the perioperative process. *Nurs Clin North Am* **32**(1): 141–151

Schreiner MS (1994) Pre-operative and post-operative fasting in children. *Pediatric Clin North Am* **41**(1): 111–20

Thornes R (1988) *Parents Staying Overnight in Hospital with their Children*. Caring for Children in the Health Service, London

Further reading

The following publications are essential reading. The first is a definitive account of the problems associated with children's consent to surgery. The second clearly outlines the responsibilities of the nurse in terms of record-keeping.

Alderson P (1993) *Children's Consent to Surgery.* Open University, Buckinghamshire

United Kingdom Central Council for Nursing, Midwifery and Health Visiting (1993) *Standard for Records and Record Keeping.* UKCC, London

4

Post-operative care

Key issues and concepts

- Transferring the care of the child from theatre to the ward

- Immediate post-operative recovery

- Principles of post-operative care

- Post-operative complications

Post-operative considerations

In the previous chapter, the importance of maintaining the physical and psychological safety of the child during the pre-operative phase of surgical care was highlighted. In post-operative care too, these issues are equally important, although the focus of care is aimed at prevention of possible complications of anaesthesia and surgical intervention; early detection where such complications arise, and the promotion of post-operative rehabilitation and preparation for discharge. Co-ordinating this care can be achieved by continued consideration of Davies and Klein's (1994) evaluative principles:

- optimising the health of the child in the period after surgery

- reducing the child and family's anxiety through teaching and planning

- planning perioperative management

- assessing post-operative health care needs for discharge and follow-up.

Optimising the health of the child in the post-operative period

During the post-operative period, children are highly dependent on nursing staff to assess both their condition and subsequent needs. Therefore, it is essential that observational and assessment skills are excellent among staff caring for children at this post-operative stage . Such skills are essential because of the risks of serious and life-threatening complications that detailed observations and assessment can help to prevent. The main aspects of care in which these skills are used are in the safe recovery from anaesthesia and detection of post-operative complications for example, airway obstruction, haemorrhage, shock and infection. As such, care must be systematically planned and include attention to such issues as well as integrating the individual needs of the child and the special care which is determined by the nature of the surgical intervention which the child has had. These concerns are relevant from the immediate post-operative period until discharge.

The immediate post-operative care of the child begins on transfer from the operating theatre to the recovery unit. At this stage, the child may be rousable, but their level of consciousness will be variable. In cases where the child is not being electively ventilated for a short period following surgical intervention, the child will be breathing spontaneously, but will not be in complete control of their airway because of the effects of the anaesthetic. Therefore, the child will not have a gag or cough reflex. This means that the child is susceptible to respiratory obstruction either by the accumulation of secretions, which if inhaled can cause aspiration pneumonia, or by the tongue, which can cause a physical barrier to inspiration and expiration. To prevent such complications, the child can be nursed in the semiprone position which is useful in encouraging the drainage of secretions from the mouth and preventing aspiration, and by using a guedel airway which, when inserted, controls the position of the tongue, thereby preventing obstruction and maintaining the patency of the airway. However, it is to be noted that the use of the semiprone position to assist the drainage of oral secretions cannot be used following all types of surgery, and that these children are even more reliant on the observational and practical skills of nursing staff to prevent aspiration occurring.

Measuring respiratory rate

As well as observing the child for signs of a physical blockage of their airway, an assessment of the efficiency of respiratory effort is also made. This is done by monitoring the rate and rhythm of respirations and listening for any unusual noises, and comparing these findings to pre-operative assessment recordings and normal ranges of respiratory rates in children.

Table 4.1: Normal ranges of respiratory rates in children

Age	Rate ·
0–1 month	30–40 resps./minute
1 month–1 year	26–40 resps./minute
1–6 years	20–30 resps./minute
6–10 years	18–24 resps./minute
10+ years	16–24 resps./minute

(Cited in Tompson and Ashwill, 1992)

In infants of up to one year it is better to watch the movement of the stomach to count the number of respirations per minute because of the slightly different mechanisms involved in the way children of this age breathe. In children over this age, the movement of the chest wall is a reliable indicator of the respiratory rate. The colour of the circum-oral area and nailbeds is checked to ensure that there is no evidence of cyanosis indicating poor oxygenation of the peripheries. This measurement can be double-checked by using an oxygen saturation monitor. Poor oxygenation is indicated by the saturation measurements of less than 94%. Nursing actions to correct such findings are firstly to check that the child's position is compatible with adequate respiratory function and that no physical blockage of the airway has occurred and secondly, administration of prescribed oxygen via face-mask, with continuous monitoring of the subsequent changes in respiratory effort and functioning using the methods already outlined. It may also be necessary to use gentle suctioning to remove any excessive oral secretions. For these reasons, oxygen and suction are always on hand in the recovery unit, and similarly, such equipment will need to be available on the ward, once transfer of the child has taken place. This kind of detailed observation is made until the child has recovered their usual conscious state following anaesthesia and is able to maintain their own airway independently.

Measuring pulse rate

Detailed observation in the immediate post-operative period is not simply confined to monitoring the child's respiratory status. Equally important is the circulatory status where the systematic measurement and recording of the child's pulse rate and blood pressure can reveal a pattern of stability, or indeed one in which there is cause for concern. Interpreting measurements of pulse rate and blood pressure means that the nurse caring for the child who has had surgery must first, understand the significance of what is being recorded and, should be able to compare these measurements to those recorded for the child in the pre-operative period and the range of normal values for children of a similar age as highlighted in *Tables 4.2 and 4.3*.

Table 4.2: Normal range of values for pulse rate in children

Age	Rate
Neonate	125–190/minute
1 month–1 year	110–160/minute
2–4 years	100–130/minute
5–10 years	90–120/minute
10+ years	65–110/minute

(As cited in Thompson and Ashwill, 1992)

Table 4.3: Normal range of values for blood pressure in children

Age	Blood Pressure (systolic)
Newborn	50–70 mmHg
1 month	70–95 mmHg
6 months	80–100 mmHg
1 year	80–100 mmHg
3 years	80–110 mmHg
6 years	80–110 mmHg
10 years +	90–120 mmHg

(As cited in Bernardo and Bove, 1993)

The pulse rate is literally a measurement of the number of times the heart beats in 1 minute. It can be recorded at a number of sites on the child's body manually, and in two main ways. For infants and small children, the most usual method is to listen to the child's heart rate using a stethoscope on the chest wall over the approximate site of the heart. This is called the apical pulse rate and is the preferred method for children in this age group because it is easier to hear the pulse rather than to rely on touch. For older children, the pulse rate can be palpated at 5 points: The carotid artery; the brachial artery; the radial artery; the femoral artery and the popliteal artery. What is felt is the wave-like movement of the artery wall as blood is forced through it. Measuring a pulse rate in this way however, gives more than a simple measure of the number of beats per minute. It is also important to feel the quality of the pulse rate for example, whether the pulse is full and bounding or rapid, weak and thready. When coupled with the measurement of the actual pulse rate, this information can provide clues about the condition of the child.

Measuring blood pressure

Generally, blood pressure is considered to be the force which is exerted by the blood on the walls of the blood vessels. Arterial blood pressure, the one which is routinely measured, is the result of the blood being forced from the left ventricle into the aorta. When this happens there is a variability in pressure in the aorta between the contraction and resting phases of the heartbeat. When the left ventricle contracts and forces blood into the aorta, this is known as the **systolic** blood pressure and is the highest of the two figures measured in blood pressure. When the heart is resting or in complete diastole, the blood pressure falls and is known as the **diastolic** blood pressure. Both measurements are quantified in terms of millimetres of mercury (mmHg) for example,

Blood pressure = $\frac{110}{75}$ mmHg

However, there are a number of elements which are necessary to maintain the blood pressure of a child:

- the cardiac output
- the circulating blood volume
- the peripheral resistance of the arterioles
- the elasticity of the artery walls
- the venous return.

The cardiac output is the amount of blood which is ejected from the heart either in each contraction or over a 1 minute period.

These aspects of the cardiac output are referred to as the stroke volume and minute volume respectively. Of particular interest is the minute volume which takes account of the rate and force of the heart's contraction and an increase in the minute volume raises both the systolic and diastolic blood pressure. However, this aspect of the blood pressure relies on the circulating blood volume. This must be kept at a near constant level in order to exert sufficient force on the walls of the arteries and subsequently maintain normal blood pressure. When large volumes of blood are lost for example, following a haemorrhage after surgical intervention, both the systolic and diastolic blood pressure will fall. Regulation of blood pressure in such circumstances is also made possible by the peripheral resistance caused by the contraction or dilation of the arterioles within the blood circulation. These very small vessels are composed entirely of smooth muscle and respond to sympathetic nervous stimulation by the vasomotor centre in the medulla oblongata. This stimulation occurs in response to the body's ability to prioritise which organs need the most blood flow according to the amount of activity. The process of contraction and dilation allows blood supply to be diverted to the organs which have the highest need during normal circumstances. However, if haemorrhage occurs following surgical intervention, peripheral arterioles will contract to ensure blood flow is diverted to priority organs, the brain and cardiac muscle itself. The elasticity of the artery walls maintains the diastolic blood pressure by providing pressure via elastic recoil following contraction of the left ventricle and the subsequent distension and collapse (recoil) of the artery that this causes. Of all the aspects of blood pressure control venous return is extremely important because it reflects the amount of blood which is being pumped through the body via the arterial and venous blood circulation. If there is insufficient venous return to the heart via the circulatory system in haemorrhage for example, then the cardiac output will decrease producing a commensurate fall in blood pressure.

When this physiological knowledge is put in to practice, it means that the nurse caring for the child in the post-operative period is able to observe and interpret any changes in the child's condition. In particular the nurse is observing for the signs of haemorrhage and shock which are two of the common complications following surgery.

Haemorrhage

Haemorrhage is a specific complication of surgery and can occur both during (*primary haemorrhage*) and after (*secondary haemorrhage*) surgical intervention. In post-operative care however, haemorrhage is observed in two ways. First, the wound site and drains where appropriate, are observed for signs of excessive bleeding. Where possible, measurements of blood draining from the wound are recorded and monitored, and the dressing covering the surgical wound are marked and the type of fluid, blood or serous leakage is observed. It is important not to remove the initial dressing from the surgical wound because of the interruption this will cause to the normal clotting process taking place underneath and to avoid early contamination of the wound itself. Instead, further dressings are applied over the original. Second, measurements of pulse rate and blood pressure are taken at more frequent intervals than they had been prior to the observation of possible haemorrhage. Initially, the pulse will rise (*tachycardia*) in an attempt by the body to compensate for a reduction in the circulating blood volume. Later signs of haemorrhage also include a falling blood pressure reading (*hypotension*) in comparison to pre-operative measurements and normal values for the age range of the child. However, haemorrhage may not always be so visible especially where there is a deep, leaking vessel under the site of the surgical intervention. In such cases, the only signs of haemorrhage may be the changes in the recordings of the child's vital sign observations and in some cases in the behaviour of the child who may become increasingly restless. Of course, such observations will need to be reported to medical staff who will then decide on an appropriate course of action.

Shock

A further complication of surgery is the clinical condition known as shock. Although there are several types of shock, the nurse caring for the child in the post-operative period needs to particularly vigilant for the signs of hypovolaemic shock. In hypovolaemic shock, the primary cause is attributable to an inadequate circulating blood volume usually as a result of haemorrhage during or after surgical intervention. Early signs of shock include:

- pallor
- clammy skin
- reduction in urine output
- tachycardia.

If left untreated, shock progresses and the child will become:

- cold and clammy
- centrally cyanosed
- hypotensive
- oliguric (little urine production).

The reasons for these observable signs of shock are found in the underlying physiological processes which take place in these circumstances.

When there is a reduction in cardiac output because of a reduced circulating blood volume, the tissues are inadequately supplied with oxygen and nutrients and the breakdown products of cell metabolism are not removed. This is particularly evident in organs which are very active and have a greater need for this function of the blood for example, the heart, brain and kidneys. Of these organs, the kidneys are especially susceptible to a reduction in blood volume and therefore perfusion hence, the readily observable reduction in urine output. When the brain tissue is affected sufficiently, the child will become restless, agitated and confused, eventually losing consciousness. The heart itself is most affected by the consequences of the inadequate supply of oxygen and removal of waste products from the general circulation which causes acidaemia. This contributes to a depression in the heart's ability to contract effectively, and therefore there is further reduction in cardiac output. Treatment for hypovolaemic shock is twofold. First, the source of the bleeding must be stemmed which may necessitate a return to theatre for ligation of leaking vessels and second, the fluid loss must be replaced which is done by administering prescribed intravenous fluids or blood products.

Measuring temperature

The purpose of measuring temperature in the post-operative period is to determine whether the child is hypo or hyperthermic and to instigate appropriate nursing measures in response to any abnormal findings. During some surgical procedures, the child's skin can be exposed to the environment for long periods which can have the effect of cooling the child significantly. If the child undergoes major bowel surgery, problems of temperature control are further compounded by exposure of the gut which also results in excessive heat loss. Theatre suites can be heated to counter the problems of intra-operative heat loss, but the nurse caring for the child in the post-operative period must observe that the child's temperature remains stable. Hyperthermia is more usually a problem in the period of 36–48 hours following surgery when such findings are an indication of infection.

Measuring a child's temperature is done at a minimum interval of 1 hour between each reading. If it is done any more frequently, changes are unlikely to be significant. There are three main methods of measuring temperature in the child. These are: orally, axillary, tympanic, although in rare cases a fourth method, rectally, can be used. When taking an oral temperature, the thermometer is put under the child's tongue and left there for a minimum of 1 minute and then removed and the reading taken. In the immediate post-operative period, this method is contraindicated because of the potential for the child to bite and break the thermometer while their conscious state and behaviour is affected by anaesthesia or strong opiate analgesia. Axillary or tympanic temperatures are recommended for this group of children. In axillary temperature recording, the thermometer needs to be left under the child's arm for at least 3 minutes. Tympanic thermometers are much quicker to use and produce almost instant results. Whichever method is chosen, it should be used consistently so that appropriate comparisons can be made between each reading.

Table 4.4: Normal ranges for temperatures in children

Method	Range
Oral	36.4–37.4°C
Axillary	35.8–36.6°C

(As cited in Tompson and Ashwill, 1992)

Returning to the children's ward

When the child is able to maintain their own airway; their post-operative condition as indicated by observation and recording of vital signs is stable, and their conscious level has returned to within normal limits, the child will be ready to **return to the ward**. It is important to understand that in accepting the child into their care, the ward nurse also accepts responsibility and accountability for any further nursing actions. Therefore, great care and attention should be given to ensuring that all aspects of care undertaken in theatre and recovery are understood and that personal assessment and observation of the child confirms written and verbal evidence about the child's condition. In the same way that ward staff communicated essential aspects of care to theatre staff in the pre-operative period by using a theatre checklist (see *Figure 4.1*), a similar chart with the same purpose is often used in the post-operative period.

Figure 4.1: Sample post-operative checklist (adapted from Smith, 1995)

Operation:		Time in recovery:

Intra-operative problems/special instructions for recovery:

Time:																Temp:
	190															41
	180															40
	170															39
	160															38
	150															37
	140															36
BP	130															35
	120															34
	110															33
	100															
Pulse	90															
	80															
	70															
	60															
	50															
	40															
	30															
Resps	20															
	10															

Figure 4.1: continued(adapted from Smith, 1995)

Circulatory observations						Intake			Output				
Time						Time	Oral	IV	Urine	Drain	Gastric	Total	
Limb													
Circulation													
Colour													
Cool													
Warmth													
Sensation													
Movement													
Other													
Wound													
Dressing													
Leakage													
Analgesia given:													

Figure 4.1: continued(adapted from Smith, 1995)

Equipment in situ post-operatively:

	Site:	
	Site:	
	Site:	
	Site:	

Accompanying child from theatre:

Case notes	Y	N
Toy/Comforter	Y	N
Other	Y	N
Other:	Y	N
Other:	Y	N

Ward information/Special post-operative instructions:

Recovery nurse signature	Airway
Time	Conscious level
Ward nurse signature	Oxygen saturation
Time	Time out of recovery

In addition to checking that all relevant aspects have been recorded by theatre staff using the post-operative checklist, there are several issues which the ward nurse must address prior to accepting the child. These include:

1. The identity of the child must be checked, and all corresponding documentation must be that of the same child for example, X-rays and case notes.

2. The ward nurse must check the child's level of consciousness for example by asking the child to respond to his/her name or a specific command.

3. The child's breathing and other vital signs should be assessed using the parameters previously outlined.

4. The recovery staff should be able to give a handover to the ward nurse about the child and their surgery which consists of a summary of:

    *   the type of operation and the length of time taken to accomplish the surgical intervention, and response to anaesthesia including whether the child has experienced any nausea or vomiting. This will need to be continually assessed because of the very common incidence of this side-effect following anaesthesia and its effect on the reintroduction of food and drinks

    *   the condition of the wound site and any evidence of post-operative bleeding. This needs to be checked by the ward nurse to establish that no sudden haemorrhage has occurred prior to return to the ward

    *   the presence of a urinary catheter and the amount of drainage which should be measured hourly. Where no urinary catheter is in situ it is important to find out whether the child has passed urine in recovery. This is because of the effect of anaesthetic drugs on the sympathetic nervous system which can cause urinary retention. Urine should normally be passed within 12 hours of surgery

- the type of drains in situ following surgery where appropriate. Where drains are present, the amount of drainage needs to be checked by the nurse receiving the child, prior to return to the ward

- the sites of any intravenous cannulae and whether these are being used or not. Additional information which should be gathered by the ward nurse includes checking the prescription sheet to ensure that the correct fluids are currently being infused; sufficient fluids are prescribed for the first few hours following surgery and the site of the cannulae for patency and signs of extravasation. Fluid balance charts also need to be completed by theatre staff prior to return to the ward

- the availability of analgesia for the child following surgical intervention. It is essential that the nurse collecting the child from theatre knows what type of analgesia has already been administered, when it was administered, what the effect or side-effects of the analgesia were on the child and whether there is provision within the prescription for further doses of analgesia to be given.

5. The ward nurse must also check any special instructions for post-operative care which have been given by the surgeon, or will be required because of the nature of the operation undertaken. Such instructions often include the type of wound closure and dressings preferred, plaster cast care, limb elevation and positioning.

Once the nurse receiving the child is satisfied that the personal assessment reveals that the child's condition is satisfactory and that all aspects of care have been recorded appropriately, the child can be escorted back to the ward. In practice, this is done with the help of a member of theatre portering staff. When the child is returning to the ward, the parents may wish to carry their child where this is appropriate. Alternatively, the child may be more comfortable on the theatre trolley. In either case, there must be provision to deal with any emergency situation which arises on this return journey. This means that oxygen and suction must be available on the trolley, together with a geudel airway of the correct size for the child, and an Ambubag. The purpose of having such pieces of equipment available is so that the nurse can begin resuscitation procedures according to current guidelines if needed. Although the event of a child collapsing on the return from theatre is a thankfully rare occurrence, the importance of having such equipment available on the return from theatre should not be underestimated.

Immediate care on the ward

When the child returns to the ward in the immediate post-operative period, the aim of care is to ensure that a safe recovery from anaesthesia and surgery is maintained. Physical safety is promoted by prior preparation of the child's bed space with necessary equipment to support post-operative care for example, oxygen and suction, drip and catheter stands, and vital sign observation devices. The position of the child's bed within the ward area is also an important consideration from a management perspective, and must facilitate ease of observation of the child at all times. This is because on immediate return to the ward, the child will still need to be observed for signs of airway obstruction, haemorrhage and shock for the reasons already stated. However, with continued stability, the interval between vital sign observation can become less frequent according to the individual child's condition.

Reducing anxiety

Maintaining the physical safety of the child is, of course, a primary issue in post-operative children's nursing. Similarly, psychological safety is also a major feature during this phase of admission. Some of these issues are dealt with in pre-operative nursing for example, preparing the child and their family for what they will see, hear, feel and touch in the post-operative period (see *Chapter 3*). However, it is also important to remember that some aspects of hospital care are just as frightening in the post-operative period as they were in the pre-operative period. Vinsintainer and Wolfer's (1975) work, the focus of which is the things that most worry children about hospitalisation, is worth special consideration because they can offer some clues about the areas of post-operative psychological care that will need attention:

- physical harm, body injury, pain, mutilation and death
- separation from parents
- the strange and unknown and possibility of surprise
- the limits of acceptable behaviour
- the loss of control, independence and autonomy.

Planning to reduce such anxieties in the post-operative period can be achieved by using many of the techniques described in *Chapter 2*, which consider cognitive and other aspects of development as they relate to preparation. Use of these techniques in the post-operative period is undertaken immediately before any procedure is carried out, clearly outlining for the child what they might see, how it might feel and what will happen afterwards. Where possible it is necessary to give the child an element of choice, for example the time and place in which the procedure will be done. Implementing such nursing actions is more likely to give the child confidence in the fact that nothing will happen without their prior knowledge, subsequently reducing fear and anxiety, as well as allowing the child to remain independent, autonomous and in control of what is happening to them. Naturally, it is still significant that parents are involved with the child in the post-operative period as much as they are able. Some parents will want to adopt a role in which they undertake much of the post-operative care themselves. Others may not want or feel able to do so. Therefore, continued partnership and negotiation is required. The very positive aspects of such parent/nurse collaboration in reducing anxiety during the post-operative phase of care, are most easily seen in the discussion surrounding parents in the recovery room.

Brown (1995) studied the perceptions of parents and recovery staff in relation to parental presence in the recovery room following anaesthesia and surgery in children. Although the findings of the study demonstrated some disparity between the perceptions of parents and recovery staff about the success of the scheme, there were some extremely beneficial effects noted for both parents and child. Parents felt that they were making a positive contribution to their child's care by being in the recovery room when their child woke up. Further, some parents in the study highlighted that they had valued being able to tell their child that they would be on hand immediately after the operation (Brown, 1995). Children too, appeared to find the presence of their parents beneficial and were visibly less anxious when accompanied by a parent in the recovery room than those children who were not.

Planning perioperative management

Reducing anxiety caused by the experience of hospitalisation is not only confined to specific measures which are aimed at improving the experience as far as possible for the child and their family. Attention to other issues in the management of post-operative care can further contribute to a reduction in child and family anxiety for example, pain control, wound healing and infection.

Pain control

Pain control is an enormous subject within the discipline of children's nursing. This is partly because of the many myths which have surrounded children's perceptions of pain, physically and psychologically, for many decades. More recently, there have been moves among children's nurses to establish a research and evidence base from which to manage pain in children. While many of the original myths still exist about children's pain and its control, the subject is now taken so seriously that multidisciplinary approaches to caring for the child in pain are now commonplace. However, there are particular difficulties which the children's nurse needs to overcome during the assessment of pain and the implementation of measures with which to ameliorate its effects.

McCaffery's (1977) often quoted definition, 'pain is whatever the experiencing person says it is, existing wherever he says it does', gives the impression of a very subjective feeling which it is difficult, and probably impossible for another person to experience in the same way. Although such a definition of the nature of pain emphasises the individual nature of the pain experience, there are still two major assumptions contained within it. First, that the child can communicate and second, that the child is believed (Carter, 1994). Clearly, this is not possible for all children to achieve for a variety of reasons which can all influence the perception of pain in the child. The nurse needs to be aware of the child's stage of cognitive and physical development, past experiences of pain and verbal ability, while other issues such as spiritual, cultural, social and psychological conventions are also implicated. Therefore, when making an assessment of pain in the child both informal and formal mechanisms should be adopted.

Informal assessment of pain in the child is achieved by using observational techniques. These include looking at the child's behaviour both generally and specifically although this type of assessment is more suggestive of pain than it is a measure of the intensity (Burr, 1987; Carter, 1994). It is also important to remember that when observing children who are thought to be in pain in this way, what is seen may be reflective of a coping mechanism instigated by the child for dealing with the pain (Carter, 1994). Examples of the way children can behave when they are in pain include non-verbal clues such as refusal to move; unusual quietness; flat affect; restlessness, and a loss of appetite (Burr, 1987). Vocal signs of pain may be crying; whimpering; sobbing or screaming (Burr, 1987). All these kinds of observations need to be viewed in the context of how the child previously behaved and whether evidence of such behaviour constitutes a change for the individual child. Where such behaviour is identified as a response to pain, documentation and description of them is a useful adjunct to a more formal assessment.

Formal methods for the assessment of pain are becoming more readily available for all age groups. Previously, school-age children and adolescents were better served than infants and young children. The reasons for this have been because very young children have extremely limited communication skills. Now, there are a range of instruments available which are designed for use with different age groups and the overall picture is much better with formal pain assessment being possible from the neonatal period to adolescence. The advantages of using a pain assessment instrument are that the child is able to provide information about their feelings, the location and the intensity of their pain. Subsequently, such information can be compared with information gathered after a pain relieving intervention has been made with the benefit that evaluation of its efficacy is possible. Standard practice in pain assessment for children is to make an assessment prior to administration of analgesia and again 20–30 minutes afterwards so that continual review and adaptation is made. Examples of some of the currently used pain assessment instruments to accomplish this objective are highlighted in *Figures 4.2, 4.3* and *4.4* .

Figure 4.2: Visual analogue scale for pain assessment

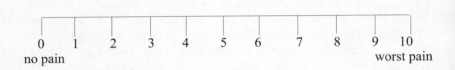

Linear pain scales like the visual analogue scale
require that children are able to distinguish
between 'no pain' at the one end of the scale and
their 'worst pain' at the other. In some cases, like
the one illustrated here, numbers are applied to
the scale, but this is only useful when the child
is numerate and understands that 10 is greater
than 1. Similarly, descriptors like 'mild hurt' or
'moderate hurt' can help the child distinguish
between different levels of intensity of pain.
This simple, but effective tool is useful for
assessing pain among a wide range of age groups.

Figure 4.3: Wong-Baker faces rating scale of pain assessment

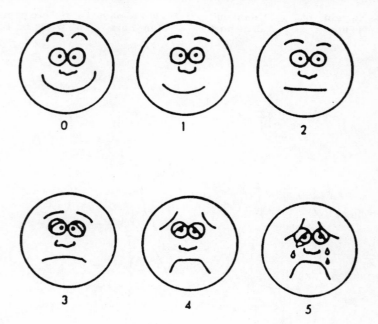

The most popular pain assessment tool for use with children is the Wong-Baker faces rating scale (Wong and Baker, 1988). In principle, the child is asked to determine which face looks like the way they are feeling. This is then used to rate the intensity of pain being felt by the child. This tool surpasses the problems encountered in using the visual analogue scale because children do not have to be able to appreciate numbers to rate their pain.

Figure 4.4: Eland color tool

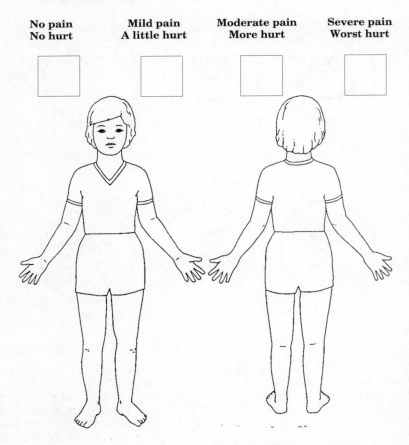

No pain No hurt	Mild pain A little hurt	Moderate pain More hurt	Severe pain Worst hurt

(Indicate child's use of right and left)

The most complex children's pain assessment tools, the Eland colour tool is unique in that it not only measures the intensity of pain, but also the site of the pain. The process of using the tool begins by the child assigning a colour to the types of pain within their experience. This is marked for reference in the boxes at the top. The child then uses the correct colour to mark the child model where they hurt. The child's use of left and right needs to be established. The tool has been used with children under the age of five with good results. However, it is a lengthy process to begin with, although the long term benefits for the child and nurse are outweighed by the reults which can be achieved.

Use of instruments like these in the post-operative period are extremely valuable, but for them to be most effective the child should be introduced to an appropriate tool in the pre-operative period.

When pain has been assessed, appropriate methods of intervention can be planned. Interventions for these purposes are varied and can be non-pharmacologically or pharmacologically based. Examples of non-pharmacological interventions that can be used in the post-operative period are guided imagery or distraction therapies as well as the use of therapeutic touch and the reassurance of a parent being close by during the post-operative period (Carter, 1994). Pharmacological methods of pain control are wid-ranging and include the use of oral medications, intravenous bolus injection or infusion and regional anaesthesia (Carter, 1994). Intramuscular injections are avoided wherever possible because of the distress this method of administration causes for children. Use of these various methods of analgesia depends on the nature and site of surgery, the acceptability of side effects and any associated medical issues which might preclude the use of certain types of analgesia for example, asthma. Therefore, choice of analgesia is determined on an individual basis.

Wound healing and infection

In elective surgery, the nature of the underlying problem requiring intervention is known. The surgeon can plan to make the incision at a site which will allow ease of access to the organ or tissue requiring surgery, reduce limitation to function in the post-operative period and will produce the best long term cosmetic effect for the child (Morison, 1992). However, while all care is taken to ensure that these factors are considered, it should be noted that for some children, the nature of the surgery they require renders the wound more susceptible to breakdown and subsequent infection. Examples of this type of 'high risk' surgical intervention are those which involve exposure of the bowel. This is because of the very large numbers of potential pathogens contained within the bowel which can cause wound infection and peritonitis (Morison,

1992). Other wounds which are susceptible to infection are those that need some kind of wound drainage system because of the risk of the development of a haematoma or infection. However, the decision to insert a wound drainage system into a surgical wound is not one which is taken lightly. This is because there is an increased risk of infection by normal commensals of the skin which have access to the wound via the drainage system itself; the tissue surrounding the drainage system is more susceptible to infection because of the presence of a 'foreign body', and the internal position of the drain can cause pressure necrosis to other organs or blood vessels which may lead to secondary haemorrhage or the formation of a fistula (Morison, 1992). Of the two major types of wound drainage systems available, 'passive' systems are the most problematic in terms of infection because they rely on gravity for their ability to drain whereas 'active' drainage systems which provide low or high pressure suction are more acceptable because these tend to be within closed drainage units. Other factors which also influence surgical wound healing are related to intra-operative cleansing and draping. Here, contamination of the wound site is minimised by the use of skin cleansing preparations as local policy dictates and covering the child with sterile drapes during the operative procedure.

Healing of a surgical wound takes place by a process called 'primary intention' or the union of the two wound edges and is shown in *Figure 4.5*.

Figure 4.5: Healing by primary intention

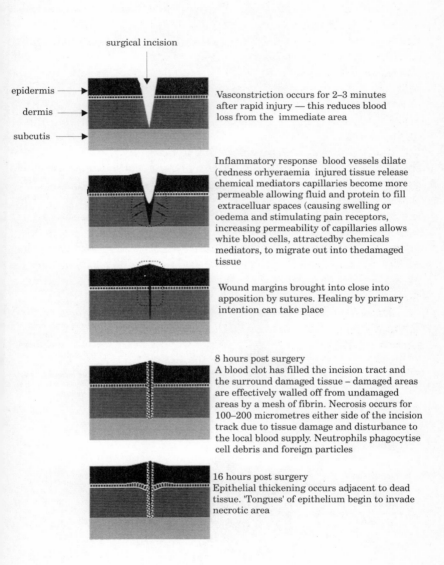

surgical incision

epidermis →

dermis →

subcutis →

Vasconstriction occurs for 2–3 minutes after rapid injury — this reduces blood loss from the immediate area

Inflammatory response blood vessels dilate (redness orhyeraemia injured tissue release chemical mediators capillaries become more permeable allowing fluid and protein to fill extracelluar spaces (causing swelling or oedema and stimulating pain receptors, increasing permeability of capillaries allows white blood cells, attractedby chemicals mediators, to migrate out into thedamaged tissue

Wound margins brought into close into apposition by sutures. Healing by primary intention can take place

8 hours post surgery
A blood clot has filled the incision tract and the surround damaged tissue – damaged areas are effectively walled off from undamaged areas by a mesh of fibrin. Necrosis occurs for 100–200 micrometres either side of the incision track due to tissue damage and disturbance to the local blood supply. Neutrophils phagocytise cell debris and foreign particles

16 hours post surgery
Epithelial thickening occurs adjacent to dead tissue. 'Tongues' of epithelium begin to invade necrotic area

Figure 4.5: continued

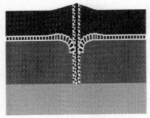

24 hours post surgery
'Tongues' of epithelium continue to advance.

The wound has poor tensile strength and is held by sutures

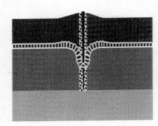

24–48 hours post surgery
Epithelial tongues unite below the level of the incision. This severs the connection between living and dead tissue effectively sealing the skin. Superficial scab (clot + dead tissue) is subsequently lost.

Maximum rate of increase in tensile strength during the first 5–12 days. Sutures no longer needed after 10–12 days.

1 week post surgery
Capillaries bud from the nearest vessels and extend loops into damaged areas. Rapid proliferation of fibroblasts and migration in the direction of capillary extension. Granulation tissue formed (primary capillaries, fibroblasts and collagen laid down by fibroblasts).

Scar tissue slowly increases in strenght due to continued deposition of collagen. It achieves a maximum of 70–80% of the original skin tensile strength.

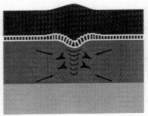

1 month post surgery
New connective tissue replaces epithelium. Thickening of skin layers may remain. White scar may form due to deposition and contraction of collagen.

Healing by primary intention is facilitated by 'primary closure' of the wound. That is to say that the union of the wound is initially undertaken by some type of closure for example, sutures, clips or staples. However, the effectiveness of these types of closure is closely related to the surgeons expertise in choosing the right kind of closure for the particular wound and using it properly. In wounds that are not closed effectively, there is a danger that the tensile strength of the wound will be insufficient and will therefore be prone to dehiscence (a breakdown in the integrity of the wound along all or part of its length); (Morison, 1992). Wound dehiscence can also occur as a result of infection. However, the children's nurse needs to be aware of earlier signs of wound infection since dehiscence is a rather late sign.

Observation of the wound site should begin immediately the child returns to the recovery room following anaesthesia. Initially, theatre staff are observing for immediate wound complications which include primary haemorrhage. As time progresses however, there is a change in emphasis in why the children's nurse is observing the wound site. The first signs of infection are progressive erythema around the site of the incision. Careful observation will reveal the extent of the erythema which, it must be appreciated, is a normal part of the healing process and is part of the body's natural immune response to injury. When observation suggests that erythema is progressive, wound infection may be suspected especially where this is accompanied by local oedema and pain. If infection is present in the deep tissues rather than within the wound itself, it is possible that a raised temperature will be the first sign of post-operative infection. In such cases, the medical staff may also want to exclude the possibility of chest or urinary tract infections before confirming the surgical site as the primary source of infection. When the wound itself is infected, there may be some evidence of exudate which needs to be swabbed and sent to the laboratory for culture and antibiotic sensitivity for correct treatment of the wound to be prescribed. In these circumstances, the child's temperature must be carefully and frequently monitored and treated with anti-pyretic drugs according to local policy until the type of bacteria causing the infection is isolated or antibiotics are prescribed in anticipation of receiving the laboratory results. If such an infection is allowed to progress, the results can be fatal. This is because the bacteria responsible for the wound infection can subsequently spread into the general circulation causing septicaemia.

Assessing health care needs

In previous discussion, the kinds of complications which have been alluded to are those which are common throughout the surgical experience for both the child and their family. In the main, these principles have been directed towards physical and psychological safety. Assessment of health care needs in the post-operative period extends these principles and requires the children's nurse to consider the specific details of post-operative care which may be required in relation to the intervention carried out. Obviously it is beyond the scope of this book to itemise all the specific post-operative care which may be needed for the various types of surgery which children could perceivably undergo. However, it is possible to suggest ways in which these specific aspects of care can be considered and such a framework is visualised in *Figure 4.6*.

Figure 4.6: Incorporating specific aspect of surgical care in the post-operative period

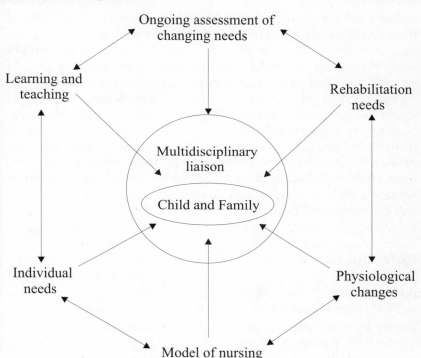

What is noticeable about this conception of post-operative care is the central issues which permeate all the surgical care planned and delivered throughout admission: partnership with the child and family and multidisciplinary collaboration and liaison.

Summary

It is clear that the post-operative care of the child following surgery is a speciality of children's nursing which calls for highly skilled and dynamic professionals. Nurses working in such specialities of children's nursing must be able to identify common and not so common complications of surgical intervention, responding quickly and appropriately to information gathered either by observation of the individual child, measurement of specific parameters or indeed a combination of both. The surgical nurse also needs to understand the underlying physiological components of the interventions made and to be able to apply such principles to the development of individualised, child centred nursing care. In addition to these qualities, work in children's surgery means that the long-term hazards of intervention must be acknowledged and ameliorated wherever possible by considering the impact of surgical intervention on the child and their family. It is clear that nursing responsibilities in post-operative care are located in ensuring that such care implemented, is based on sound evidence, research and rationales and contributes to both the physical and psychological care of the child.

References

Bernardo LM, Bove M (1993) *Pediatric Emergency Nursing Procedures*. Jones and Bartlett, Boston

Brown V (1995) Parents in recovery: parental and staff attitudes. *Paediatr Nurs* **7**(7): 17–19

Burr S (1987) Pain in childhood *Nurs* **24**: 890–7

Carter B (1994) *Child and Infant Pain Principles of Nursing Care Management*. Chapman and Hall, London

Davis JL, Klein RW (1994) Perioperative care of the pediatric trama patient *AORN Journal* **60**(4): 559, 561, 563–5

McCaffery M (1977) Pain relief for the child *Pediatr Nurs* **3**(4): 11–6

Morison MJ (192) *A Colour Guide to the Nursing Management of Wounds*. Mosby Yearbook Europe, London

Smith F (1995) *Children's Nursing in Practice The Nottingham Model*. Blackwell Science, Oxford

Thompson ED, Ashwill JW (1992) *Pediatric Nursing An Introductory Text Sixth Edition*. WB Saunders, Philadelphia

Vinsintainer MA, Wolfer JA (1975) Psychological preparation for surgical pediatric patients: the effect on children's and parent's stress responses and adjustment *Pediatr* **56**:187–202

Further reading

The publications below provide some useful perspectives of children's pain and the ways in which pain assessment has developed in recent years. Recommended reading for anyone who has a keen interest in children's pain assessment.

Eland JM (1990) Pain in children *Nurs Clins North Am* **25**(4): 871–84

Jerrett M, Evans K (1988) Children's pain vocabulary *J Adv Nurs* **11**: 403–8

5

Special groups: the newborn

Key issues and concepts

+ Reasons for surgical intervention in the newborn

+ Physiological problems of the newborn

+ Preparing parents for surgery to their baby

+ Health care considerations in the pre- and post-operative periods

Identification of special groups

In the previous chapters, the general principles of caring for the child undergoing surgery have been discussed at length. While many of the principles of surgical nursing identified are applicable to most age-ranges, there are three groups for whom special consideration is needed: The newborn, the child receiving day case surgery and the child needing emergency surgery. These groups are rendered particularly vulnerable either because of their unique stage of development or because of the circumstances in which their surgery is carried out. In the next three chapters the special needs of these groups will be explored and actions which the children's nurse can instigate as part of a planned approach to care will be discussed.

Problems for the newborn

The major reasons which necessitate surgical intervention in the newborn are often related to the presence of a congenital abnormality. Some of these abnormalities are not at all life threatening and surgical intervention can be postponed until the child is sufficiently mature to withstand the stress of surgery. For other babies, a congenital abnormality represents a threat to life and surgical correction needs to take place immediately. However, the younger the infant the greater the risk in the surgical procedure because of the immaturity in physiological functioning. A premature baby requiring surgery means that there are further problems of immaturity. Therefore, in surgical intervention among all infants, immaturity of physiological functioning is a major feature which affects the type of surgical care delivered.

Optimising the health of the child in the period before surgery

In neonatal surgery there is a core group of needs which has to be addressed pre-operatively regardless of the baby's underlying condition for example, fluid and electrolyte imbalance; nutritional state; temperature control and the prevention of infection. Where surgery is performed as a life saving measure, there may be additional elements of care that need to be considered such as airway maintenance and cardiovascular support. All these aspects pre-operative nursing the newborn must be considered in conjunction with both the general principles of care discussed in *Chapter 3,* and the special nursing management considerations dictated by the individual needs of the baby and the underlying condition requiring surgery.

Fluid and electrolyte imbalance

Consideration of normal anatomy in the newborn reveals that kidney function in terms of regulating fluid and electrolyte balance is inefficient particularly in the neonatal period. At birth, the kidney is unable to excrete an excess fluid load, and urine cannot be sufficiently concentrated to conserve fluid in periods of dehydration (Johnston, 1994). In spite of these excretory and regulatory problems, the term infant can conserve sodium. This means that if feeds or intravenous fluids are given that have a high concentration of sodium, the baby is at risk of hypernatraemia (high sodium level in the blood) which can cause damage to the brain. It is imperative that fluid and electrolyte balance is monitored closely. It is also important to remember that the action of some drugs can be altered by renal function immaturity and that dosages may be altered accordingly (Johnston, 1994). Nursing actions involved in ensuring that fluid and electrolyte balance are maintained in the pre-operative period include accurate recording and completion of fluid charts (input and output), and safe administration of any prescribed fluids via the intravenous route using a continuous infusion pump. Oral, and alternative methods of feeding are also recorded on the fluid balance chart. However, neonates are also fasted prior to surgery which raises a similar debate to the fasting of older children prior to surgery. In general, if a baby is being breast fed this can be done within 2–3 hours of planned transfer to theatre, although with bottle or enterally fed babies this fasting time may be increased to 3–4 hours depending on local preference. This discrepancy occurs because of the differing composition of breast and other types of oral feeding.

Nutritional state

The normal, term baby is born being able to suck and swallow almost immediately and with digestive enzymes which are active (Johnston, 1994). In more immature infants, this picture is different with less development of the gastrointestinal tract. However, in cases where feeding is not established either because of an underlying physiological problem or the immediate need for surgery, nutritional status must be maintained by artificial means. This is because the infant requires energy for growth, tissue repair and to prevent metabolic complications which are associated with an inadequate calorific intake. Unfortunately, there are difficulties associated with artificial methods of feeding that are particularly related to the problems of delivery of enteral or parenteral feeding systems and loss of the normal reflex to suck. In the sick newborn baby, enteral feeds may not be tolerated because of poor gut motility (Linnett, 1996) while there are problems associated with extravasation of peripheral intravenous cannula sites when these are used for the administration of parenteral feeding. If artificial feeding methods are needed, it is possible to encourage the baby to practice sucking by using a dummy. This familiarises the baby with the feeling of fullness associated with feeding, although this method can only be used when the infant is receiving enteral nutrition, with the purpose of preventing the loss of the reflex to suck during the transition to learned feeding actions (Orr and Allen, 1986).

Temperature control

The temperature regulation mechanism of the neonate is far less well developed than in older children. Neonates also have a disproportionately large surface area to body mass and as such, they are at risk of losing heat by evaporation, conduction, radiation or convection. When the environmental temperature is unstable, the baby's physiological response is to use stores of fat and increase the metabolic rate to adjust temperature when cold. This has the effect of increasing oxygen demand which, for a baby who may already have respiratory difficulty, compounds the problem. Therefore, in the pre-operative care of the neonate requiring surgery, it is essential that the baby's temperature is kept as stable as possible. This effect can be achieved with clothing and wrapping and where the baby is particularly vulnerable, incubators and radiant heaters can be used.

Prevention of infection

The term infant is especially susceptible to infection because of their immature immune system (Glasper and Campbell, 1995; Philip, 1996). In neonates, the poor development of specific and non-specific immune responses means that there is a limited response to infection with a commensurate dissemination within the body (Johnston, 1994; Philip, 1996). This is because the immaturity of the immune system renders it difficult for localisation of the source of infection to take place, leading to many more generalised symptoms that are often difficult to discern from symptoms of other problems in the neonatal period. Philip (1996) suggests these include:

- lethargy
- poor feeding
- temperature instability
- unexplained cyanosis
- diarrhoea
- vomiting.

The neonate is at risk of acquiring infection at several stages:

1. Across the placenta during late pregnancy (Glasper and Campbell, 1995)

2. During delivery by direct contact with organisms present in the vagina (Glasper and Campbell, 1995; Johnston, 1996)

3. In the weeks following birth from self-infection via the umbilical stump, or through invasion of other sites such as the eyes, nose, skin, respiratory system and the gastrointestinal and genitourinary systems (Glasper and Campbell, 1995; Philip,1996).

However, the neonate requiring surgery is more susceptible to infection because of their presenting condition, their reliance on equipment provided within the hospital for example, incubators, suction apparatus and intravenous infusion sites as well as additional wound sites and drainage mechanisms used in the post-operative period and the potential for cross-infection from one infant to another during hospitalisation. Therefore, it is essential that the children's nurse is absolutely scrupulous about cleanliness of equipment used and that personal hygiene during caring for such infants is exact to reduce the associated risks as far as possible, but where symptoms of infection become apparent, these should be reported immediately so that appropriate treatment can be started.

In the post-operative period too, these aspects of nursing care are also important and play an equally significant role in the planning and delivery of care for the baby. As with all types of surgery, post-operative care is also guided by specific needs associated with the procedure undertaken and will need to be incorporated into the care plan. In the same way that these needs were highlighted in *Chapter 4*, post-operative nursing care for the neonate can be similarly considered.

Reducing anxiety

The nature of some conditions requiring surgery in the neonatal period means that there may be a necessity to transfer the baby to a specialist unit for surgical repair and post-operative care. As a result of this, the parents and child are separated which can interfere with the normal bonding and attachment processes which take place after the child's birth. The serious nature of some congenital abnormalities also contributes to difficulties in the bonding and attachment process between some parents and their baby. In addition, there are often attendant anxieties about the baby's condition, diagnosis and prognosis and the possible causes of the type of abnormality present. Therefore, the major considerations of nursing care in these circumstances are the promotion and encouragement of parent/child bonding and attachment, and reducing anxieties which can be caused by the baby's treatment and condition. One of the most useful ways to consider these factors is by using Purcell's (1996) categories of informational need:

- knowledge about the procedures that the child has to undergo
- warning about changes in the child's appearance
- knowledge about changes in their child's behaviour
- knowing about the ward environment.

Knowledge about the procedures that the child has to undergo

In *Chapter 2*, the nature of information giving and the role it plays in reducing parental fear and anxiety were outlined. In these special circumstances too, the importance of consistent, frequent and honest explanation is no less important. Parents need to know about the proposed surgery and the reasons underpinning the need for it to be carried out. However, as Glasper and Campbell (1995) assert, this kind of information should be free from medical jargon and given according to the parents' ability to assimilate what they are being told.

Changes in the child's appearance

As the baby is prepared for theatre and in the post-operative period there can be significant changes to their appearance. Parents need to be prepared for these changes and, wherever it is possible, should be involved in caring for their baby to the level they feel appropriate. Methods which can be used to prepare parents for these changes are using photographs and diagrams which explain essential elements of the procedure. Where possible, it can be useful to introduce other parents whose baby has experienced a similar intervention.

Behavioural changes

In *Chapter 2*, the problems associated with a change in the child's behaviour were singled out as being the primary effects of the surgical experience about which parents needed to know. In the case of the neonate receiving surgery, the problems are less about how the child will behave and more about the ways in which the child will not behave before or following surgery. Parents anticipate the things that their newborn infant is likely to be able to do and the ways in which they will be able to respond to their needs. When a baby is referred for surgical intervention in the period after birth there are likely to be changes in what can be accomplished in response to the need for surgical intervention. Therefore, parents will need to be advised about changes they can expect in terms of what responses the baby will make and how they can still interact with their newborn child albeit in a different kind of way to that which was expected. This kind of preparation can be used to encourage parents to maintain physical and social contact with their baby with the effect that they are encouraged to continue to bond with their infant and continue the process of attachment (Glasper and Campbell, 1995; Purcell, 1996).

The environment

In both the pre- and post-operative periods, the baby may be transferred to a neonatal surgical unit. This can be a very frightening experience for parents who may never have contemplated what the inside of such a unit could look like. In some institutions, it is possible for the parents to visit the neonatal unit prior to delivery of their baby where it is known that surgical intervention will be required. For those parents who were not expecting such circumstances, it can be very reassuring to be shown around the unit when they arrive. In both cases, the equipment being used to monitor the baby's condition can be explained according to need, but it is more important to encourage the parents to touch, stroke and caress their baby as much as possible (Purcell, 1996).

Planning perioperative management

Planning perioperative management of the neonate requiring surgery is largely dependent on the type of facilities which are available at the hospital where baby is born. For some infants this will mean that transfer to another hospital is inevitable because more appropriate facilities are available elsewhere. When such situations arise, preparation for transfer needs to include not only an account of the physical safety of the baby, but also the way in which parents will be able to accompany their child. Preparation for this experience, and reducing anxieties caused by the delivery of a baby requiring highly intensive care also needs to be accomplished by thorough assessment of the baby and family's needs and promoting partnership with nursing staff in caring for the sick infant. Overall, nursing care of neonates requiring surgery is guided by their individual needs, whilst accounting for the special considerations of care which relate to the immaturity of their physiological functioning and the surgery which is proposed and subsequently received. In attending to these needs, the importance of the principles of pre- and post-operative care, physical and psychological, should not be forgotten since they contribute greatly to perioperative management (See *Chapters 3* and *4*).

Assessing health care needs

As with other groups of children requiring surgery, assessment of health care needs is ongoing and should be addressed from the time of admission, through treatment, discharge and beyond. For families whose child has needed intensive treatment, there can be many fears associated with the thought of discharge back to the family home. These are generally related to the parents' feelings about their ability to cope with infant's needs and the worry about complications that may arise at home. Careful explanation about these issues as well as the appropriate construction of opportunities for learning and teaching to take place all have a role in building the confidence of parents as they prepare for discharge (See *Chapter 10*). These kinds of learning and teaching opportunities may need to be related to basic child care skills or to more technical aspects of care that may be required for example, stoma care. Liaison with appropriate community staff can begin early in the period of hospitalisation so that secure relationships are made between the family and nursing staff in preparation for discharge. Where health promotion needs are identified for either the baby or the family, these can be addressed on an ongoing basis throughout admission.

Summary

The special needs of neonates undergoing surgery and their families are enormous and complex. However, with an organised approach to care which accounts for physiological differences between the newborn and other groups of children, the application of principles related to pre- and post-operative surgery and the specific needs of the child which are dictated by condition and the need for surgery, the impact of a partnership between the family and nursing staff can be used to great effect. This, of course, calls for a great depth of skill among children's nurses caring for the neonate requiring surgery so that early complications are observed and treated, the well-being of the baby and their family is promoted and the impact of a period of hospitalisation so soon after birth is minimised.

References

Glasper EA, Campbell S (eds) (1995) *Whaley and Wong's Children's Nursing.* Mosby, London

Johnston PGB (1994) *Vulliamy's The Newborn Child* 7th Edition. Churchill Livingstone, Edinburgh

Linnett S (1996) The special care baby unit. In: McQuaid L, Huband S, Parker E eds. *Children's Nursing.* Churchill Livingstone, London

Orr MJ, Allen SS (1986) Optimal oral experiences for infants on long-term total parental nutrition. *Nutrition in Clinical Practice* 9: 288–95

Philip AGS (1996) *Neonatalogy A Practical Guide.* WB Saunders, Philadelphia

Purcell C (1996) Preparation of school-age children and their parents for intensive care following surgery. *Intensive Care and Critical Care Nursing* **12**(4): 218–25

Further reading

These texts are comprehensive and wide-ranging and as such, are extremely useful for gathering an overall picture of neonatal care.

Halliday HL, McClure G, Reid M (1989) *Handbook of Neonatal Intensive Care* 3rd Edition. Balliere Tindall, London

Robertson NRC (1988) *A Manual of Normal Neonatal Care.* Hodder and Stoughton, London

6

Day case surgery

Key issues and concepts

- The need for and development of children's day case surgery

- Advantages, disadvantages and suitability for day case surgery

- Nursing management of children requiring day case surgery

- Parental responsibility for children's pre- and post-operative care

---

The need for children's day case surgery

The history and development of the knowledge base which now supports the need for day case surgery for children is well recorded and easily traced. In 1959, the recommendations of the Platt Report were made known and suggested that children's admission to hospital should be avoided wherever possible, with care at home by the general practitioner becoming more usual. In 1976, The Court Report reiterated these recommendations, further arguing that if admission to hospital should be deemed to be necessary, its length should be kept to an absolute minimum. The relevance of these recommendations is apparent especially in the light of the emerging evidence of the time, that children could potentially suffer a great deal when they are separated from their families and usual routines (see *Chapters 1* and *2*). Therefore, recognition of the emotional costs of hospitalisation for children and their families lead to an increase in the consideration of children as candidates for day case surgical intervention. Such decisions to change practice have also been supported by technological advances in the provision of anaesthesia for children as well as the development of surgical techniques requiring minimal intervention. Evaluation of the effects of provision of these services has been undertaken in recent years by both the Audit Commission (1990) and National Health Service Management Executive (1991) and findings from both these studies generally indicates that in terms of value for money, day case surgery is competitive in reducing last minute cancellations; waiting lists; post-operative complications and infection. For families, there is reduced financial cost in supporting a day rather than long admission to hospital for their child with the commensurate emotional risks being decreased for the entire family (Smith, 1995). Such global benefits are now widely acknowledged with the result that at present, the focus of activity is not in proving that day case surgery is appropriate for children, but that standards are set to ensure that the quality of care continues to improve (Thornes, 1991).

Optimising the health of the child before surgery

The advantages and disadvantages of day case surgery are well defined (see *Table 6.1*), but it must be remembered that this type of surgery is not always appropriate for all children.

Table 6.1: Advantages and disadvantages of day case surgery

Advantages	Disadvantages
• Decreased psychological consequences of hospitalisation	• Parents *must* take responsibility for pre- and post-operative aspects of care
• Less disruption to family life caused by admission to hospital	• Child may not be well enough to go home giving rise to overnight stay
• Reduced cost to health authority	
• Admission arranged for a mutually convenient date	• Three trips to hospital for family
• Reduction in post-operative complications.	• Failure to arrive on time on the day
	• Parents responsible for detecting post-operative complications.

In the main, day case surgery is appropriate for children whose parents are willing to take the responsibility for their children within hours of completion of the surgical intervention. Where this kind of parental acceptance and co-operation does not exist, there is little point in considering this type of surgery because of the additional anxiety it can pose for both the child and the family (James, 1995). The kind of intervention is also an important consideration. Minor surgery such as examinations under anaesthetic (EUA); dental surgery; ophthalmic surgery; ear, nose and throat surgery (usually excepting tonsillectomy); minor orthopaedic surgery and some types of minor abdominal and genito-urinary surgery are usually regarded as suitable (James, 1995). However, The Royal College of Surgeons (1992) suggest that if surgery is likely to take in excess of one hour, the case is not suitable to be done on a day basis. Other children who are more likely to be considered to be unsuitable for day case surgery are premature babies, all infants under 5kg and those children who have a history of having had an upper respiratory tract infection within two weeks of the date of surgery (James, 1995).

Planning perioperative management

In day case surgery, the turnover of patients is very high, and it can be an extremely stressful environment in which to work. However, James (1995) points out that in spite of the demands of the environment, day case surgery is a very challenging and rewarding speciality with the opportunity to follow children through from admission to discharge. To achieve such complete care for children and their families, planning perioperative management in day case surgery is highly organised. This level of organisation begins with thorough preparation of the child and the family.

When children are considered to be suitable candidates to receive day case surgery, preparation procedures are instigated using the parameters described in *Chapter 2* and are dependent upon the nature of the surgical intervention as well as the age and cognitive development of the child. Parents too, need to have sufficient preparation where day case surgery is the treatment of choice, since their co-operation is required throughout the time from planning the event to complete recovery. In particular, parents need to know about the procedure itself, how to reassure and support their child between the pre-admission visit and the day of the operation, together with a clear outline of what will be expected of them for example, the importance of fasting their children prior to admission on the day of surgery. Co-operation on the latter issue is unequivocal, especially where the child is admitted for surgery on the morning list. In day case surgery, the times of fasting are the same as those for other elective procedures, 6 hours for solid food and 2–3 hours for juice or breast milk. Therefore, as part of the preparation programme for admission it is essential that these issues are discussed with the child's parents and that understanding of the importance of adhering to the stated guidelines is understood. It is also pertinent to give any information associated with the child's discharge at this time to allow parents to read through the material prior to admission. This is done so that parents have the opportunity to check that they understand all that is being required of them and to formulate any further questions they may have regarding the procedure or discharge.

Assessment begins at pre-admission clinic where the nursing history is taken and any medical investigations which are needed before surgery are performed and recorded. On admission, the same principles of pre-operative care discussed in *Chapter 3* apply because the intention is still to maintain the physical and psychological safety of the child. Where differences occur, they are usually in the type of pre-medication and anaesthetic given to the child which are both short acting because of the need for a quick recovery with minimum side-effects in the post-operative period.

In the post-operative period itself, care principles are based on the same considerations discussed in *Chapter 4*. However, the short-acting anaesthetics used in day cases, coupled with the minimal length of general anaesthesia means that children will make a far quicker recovery than when more major surgery with a longer anaesthetic is undertaken. Therefore, post-operative care is adjusted according to the nature of the procedure undertaken, the speed of recovery and the kind of information which is needed by the child and the family.

Reducing anxiety

As previously described, there are many similarities between the principles of pre- and post-operative care for children receiving either elective day case or in-patient surgery. However, particular differences between the two methods of elective surgery arise when considering the detailed knowledge that parents will need to have in the post-operative period. Examples of this type of knowledge occurs where the child has had a surgical incision and needs pain control. Parents will need to be told about two aspects of care. Firstly, how to observe their child's wound for signs of healing and what they should do if signs of infection become apparent. Second, parents should also know what to do about pain control for their child since this remains an issue in day case surgery in spite of the relatively minor nature of the surgical interventions undertaken on this basis. However, it is still imperative that appropriate methods of analgesia are administered to the child and that parents know what to do about continuing appropriate analgesia when they are at home. Parents should also know how to contact the hospital if they are worried about any aspect of their child's care in the post-operative period.

Assessing health care needs

For families whose children are undergoing day case surgery, there are a number of potential fears and anxieties associated with both the procedure and discharge from hospital following its completion, not least of which pertain to the responsibility parents agree to take for their child's health care before and after discharge. In assessing health care needs then, it is important to bear these issues in mind and to give information to and offer appropriate teaching opportunities for parents that account for both pre-and post-operative care outcomes (see *Chapter 10*).

Summary

In terms of principles of pre- and post-operative care, there are very few differences between elective surgery as a day case or in-patient. Where significant differences do occur, they are found in the type of preparation which is offered to parents to enable them to care for their child within a few hours of surgical intervention. Here, informational needs are paramount. This is because it is essential that parents comply with guidelines offered in the pre-operative period where much of the responsibility for preparing the child physically for surgery falls to them. Similarly, in the post-operative period, parents must have sufficient informational resources at their disposal. Careful preparation of parents in this kind of intervention can ensure that the need for lengthy admission is avoided with the result that the child suffers fewer consequences of hospitalisation.

References

Audit Commision (1990) *A Shortcut to Better Services: Day Surgery in England and Wales*. The Audit Commision, London

Court Report (1979) *Fit for the Future: The Report of the Commitee of Child Health Services*. HMSO, London

James J (1995) Day care admissions *Paediatr Nurs* **7**(1):25–9, 37

NHSME (1991) *Day Surgery: Making it Happen*. HMSO, London

Platt Report (1959) *The Welfare of Children in Hospital*. HMSO, London

Royal College of Surgeons of England (1992) *Guide for Day Case Surgery*. Royal College of Surgeons, London

Smith F (1995) *Children's Nursing in Practice the Nottingham Model*. Blackwell Science, Oxford

Thornes R (1991) *Just for the Day*. National Association for the Welfare of Children in Hospital, London

Further reading

Ling J (1996) Day case provision in adistrict general hospital. *Paediatr Nurs* **8**(6): 25–28

Spicher C, Yund C (1989) Effects of preadmission preparation on compliance with homecare instructions *J Pediatr Nurs* **4**(4): 255–62

7

Emergency surgery

Key issues and concepts

• The need for emergency admission for surgery

• Physical care and assessment of the child admitted via the emergency route

• Informational needs of parents and their children

• Planning emergency surgical care

Background to emergency care

Children who need emergency care and their families demand a high degree of physical and psychological care from those health care professionals with whom they come into contact. These health care professionals need to be able to mobilise effective observational, preparation and caring skills so that the impact of an emergency admission is minimised. Equally in a short space of time, a therapeutic relationship needs to be established where the needs of both the child and family are identified and planning of subsequent care is started. As with all other children who require surgery, the main aims of this type of care are directed towards maintaining the physical and psychological safety of the child in partnership with families.

Children are admitted to hospital as surgical emergencies for many reasons. These range from trauma and accidents at the most serious, abdominal symptoms that may need medical evaluation and subsequent intervention, to cases where foreign bodies like beads and sweets need to be surgically removed under anaesthetic. Whatever the problem, nursing care must be well planned and delivered and take account of the special needs of this very vulnerable group of children. However, the present problems in children's emergency care means that the environmental characteristics of the units to which children are admitted are not always able to meet the special needs with which they are presented. Although children's casualty departments do exist, the majority of children admitted to hospital as an emergency will not have the luxury of this experience where expert children's nurses and doctors are in attendance. More often, children admitted as an emergency visit a predominantly adult oriented casualty department. The situation is getting better and more hospitals are recognising the importance of having appropriately trained staff to care for children's emergencies. Consequently, special rooms have been set up for children so that they are cared for away from the noise and bustle of the main treatment areas. This means that the fears and anxieties which children experience in such situations can be reduced and the possible psychological effects of an emergency admission on the child are minimised.

Optimising the health of the child before surgery

As previously suggested, there are a variety of conditions that necessitate a child to be admitted to hospital for emergency surgery. The nature of the condition will determine both the type and extent of stabilisation procedures which are implemented, suggesting whether physical or psychological care is the priority.

Physical care

When the physical condition of the child is poor on arrival in hospital, the main concerns of emergency staff are management of the child's airway, breathing and circulation. These elements of normal physiological functioning have to be assessed and stabilised before surgery can be considered. First the child's airway must be patent which means first checking that there are no mechanical obstructions like vomit or oral secretions for example. Second, an assessment of the child's breathing pattern will be made. This includes similar aspects of assessment to those discussed in relation to post-operative care: rate rhythm, noise and effort. Changes in these assessments need to be reported to medical staff immediately who will then decide on an appropriate course of action. The third consideration is the child's circulatory status. Where there is obvious haemorrhage or reason to suspect that the child has some internal bleeding, vital sign observations give important clues about the child's condition. These need to monitored very closely and changes documented and reported. Depending on the results of this type of immediate physical assessment, the child may need medical interventions ranging from ventilatory support to management of the circulating blood volume via intravenous access. However, immediate assessment and intervention do not end at this point and children can be subjected to a whole barrage of tests and procedures to evaluate their condition. Other important areas of nursing assessment include the child's level of consciousness; temperature and signs of hypothermia or fever; pain including site, type, intensity and duration as well as the instigation of appropriately considered measures to relieve or alleviate it. Where it is clear that the child will go to theatre imminently, other aspects of pre-operative care are instigated. This can be achieved by using the pre-operative checklist as a guide to physical care with the additional advantage that it provides a quick and easy reference to essential information for theatre staff. The child will be fasted from admission to casualty and the time of the last meal will be established so that the anaesthetist can provide appropriate safety measures at induction of anaesthesia. Alternatively, where surgical intervention can be delayed, the required period of time can be allowed to elapse before the child is taken to theatre. Consent is an issue to which attention must also be directed in this kind of admission. As previously stated in *Chapter 3*, the child can be taken to theatre without parental consent having been given if the child's condition is life threatening. However, wherever possible, emergency staff will go to great lengths to locate parents so that they can be asked to give their consent for the surgical procedure to be undertaken.

It is important to remember that these kinds of emergency measures will not be appropriate for all children who arrive in casualty, and that some children will not need the highly intensive care discussed above. However, all children must be assessed thoroughly on their arrival at hospital, and on the basis of the initial assessment, care appropriate to the condition of the child can be planned and implemented. For some children this may mean going to theatre from the accident and emergency department and returning to the ward following recovery from anaesthesia. For others, there may be a period of observation on the children's ward before the decision to undertake a surgical intervention is made. This is often the case where there is inconclusive evidence to support immediate surgery for example, a possible appendicitis. For others, transfer to the ward takes place to facilitate preparation for theatre or where surgery can wait until the end of the planned theatre list. Whatever type of route is planned for the child to go to theatre, there are significant nursing concerns related to the psychological preparation of the child and the family. This is because for many children, their first experience of hospital is as a result of an emergency admission.

Reducing anxiety

The concerns of children and their families are quite different in an emergency situation from elective or day case surgery. Therefore the kinds of measures which are implemented to assist families to cope with admission must reflect the change in the nature of the sources of anxiety.

Muller *et al* (1992) reported that the key issues for families are found in their anxieties about handing over the care of their child to hospital staff; the role which is played by guilt about the cause of admission especially where parents perceive that they could have instigated actions to avoid the need for hospitalisation; the welfare of other children at home, and the prospects of their child's survival following surgical intervention however minor the procedure appears to be to health care staff. For children, the only reliable source of information about their worries during an emergency admission can be gleaned from Vinsintainer and Wolfer's (1975) study about the things which worry children when they go into hospital. It is also possible to suggest that the anxiety experienced by parents can be important to the way in which children respond to their admission, and here the notion of contagious anxiety is an important consideration. Ameliorating the effects of an emergency admission requires that nursing staff are aware of the asset which parents can be in situations like these as well as the integral role parents can play in the subsequent reduction of anxiety felt by their child.

Melynck (1994) examined different kinds of intervention which nurses could make to enable parents to assist in caring for their children who had been admitted as emergency cases. What is clear from the findings of this study are that there are two kinds of information which parents need to help them cope with such an admission. The first type of information which is needed is related to the child's likely behaviours both during admission and following discharge. The second type of information to which parents respond positively is related to the nature of their parenting role while they are in hospital with their child. The results of the study demonstrated that parents coped better with unplanned admission, if they were given information about both of these aspects. Mothers who were given this type of information increased their participation their child's care and had a better repertoire of coping mechanisms because they knew what to expect from their child. Similarly, when followed up after a period of unplanned hospital admission, mothers cared better for their children at home because of the confidence which they had developed during hospitalisation and the relatively 'safe' environment where they could ask questions if they were unsure. Other benefits for parents and children in this study were found to be in the better support that parents could give when they knew about the nature and purpose of the procedure. This helped to reduce the anxiety felt by the parent and in turn there was a commensurate reduction in the level of anxiety passed on to the child. Quite clearly then, there is a need to involve parents from the outset when the child is admitted as an emergency.

For children themselves, Vinsintainer and Wolfer (1975) highlight five major concerns which are relevant to most children in this situation:

1. Physical harm, body injury, pain, mutilation and death

2. Separation from parents

3. The strange and unknown and possibility of surprise

4. The limits of acceptable behaviour

5. The loss of control, independence and autonomy.

Therefore, in attempting to reduce anxiety evoked by these factors, nursing staff must take account of the child's understanding of the purpose of admission, together with their stage of cognitive development. In practice, this means that all equipment, procedures, sights, sounds and smells must be explained to the child in the most appropriate way (see *Chapter 2*). For some children preparation immediately before the procedure/intervention takes place is the optimum timescale, but for other children frequency of interventions can be distressing. Therefore, nurses must be guided by the amount and intensity of information which the child can assimilate, and the ability of parents to assist in telling their children about what is going to happen. In addition, it is important that the amount of health care staff introduced to the child is kept to a minimum. This is because consistency in caring for the child can help in the development of a trusting relationship in which the child realises that things will always be explained to them and that nothing will happen without them being told.

Perioperative management

The principles of perioperative management are extensively discussed in *Chapters 3* and *4* and, in the main, these remain the guiding principles for emergency surgery with the additional consideration of stabilisation procedures and the preparation of both the child and family for emergency surgery. As with all types of admission to hospital, nursing care must be developed from a thorough assessment of the child which informs planning and delivery of care together with evaluation and re-assessment of care activities where necessary. For the child requiring emergency surgery, this process may be rather more speedily accomplished with the result that there is often rather less time to undertake preparatory interventions than would be ideal.

Assessing health care needs

Once the nature of the surgical intervention is determined, it is then possible to develop a plan to meet the health care needs of the child and family. This includes the broad range of specific post-operative care which may be required. In addition, the children's nurse must also consider the kind of community liaison which might be appropriate to assist the child's recovery once they have been discharged from hospital. Where there is evidence to suggest that health promotion opportunities exist, this can begin in hospital and be continued either by the health visitor or school nurse. Learning and teaching aspects of admission should also be considered especially where it is clear that parents will need to provide a certain level of care when the child is discharged. The benefits of early liaison and intervention are discussed more thoroughly in *Chapter 10*.

Summary

Caring for children who require surgery as an emergency is a highly skilled aspect of children's surgical care. Nurses who are responsible for children's care during such admissions need to be able to quickly develop a relationship with the child and family which will allow appropriate urgent preparation and planning to begin. Preparation of this vulnerable group of children and their parents is an essential aspect of care and children's nurses must understand the importance of ensuring that wherever possible acceptable measures are taken to reduce the impact of this type of admission. Equally, the nurse must have highly developed observational skills to detect any changes in the child's condition which suggests the need for further medical intervention while being able to attend to the pre- and post-operative principles of care that are demanded by the child and the family.

References

Muller DL, Harris PJ, Wattley L *et al* (1992) *Nursing Children Psychology, Research and Pracitce* 2nd Edition. Chapman and Hall, London

Vinsintainer MA, Wolfer JA (1975) Psychological preparation for surgical pediatric patients: the effect on children's and parent's stress responses and adjustment. *Pediatr* **56**: 187–202

Melynck BM (1994) Coping with unplanned childhood hospitalization: Effects of informational interventions on mothers and children. *Nursing Research* **43**(1): 50–55

8

Perioperative death

Key issues and concepts

• Legal considerations following the death of a child

• The range of emotional responses to the death of a child

• The impact of family circumstances on the berevement response

Children and perioperative death

The death of a child in the perioperative period is, thankfully, very rare. However, the majority of deaths which do occur are usually related to the child's condition prior to surgery where there are injuries or abnormalities so serious that it is impossible to save life even with surgical intervention and medical support. In a number of other cases, the underpinning reasons for perioperative death are more ominous and are related to the lack of skill possessed by the 'occasional' children's anaesthetist or surgeon. Therefore, the current recommendations of the Royal College of Surgeons (1992) indicate that there should be special facilities and resources available for children's surgery. These recommendations include:

• calls for a reduction in the number of operations that are undertaken by non-specialist paediatric surgeons

- where training in children's surgery takes place, that supervision of trainees is a main priority

- no trainee children's surgeon should ever operate alone without the express permission of their consultant.

In spite of these recommendations and their continued implementation, children still die in the perioperative period. When this type of death occurs it is a traumatic experience for all individuals involved, and the associated depth and breadth of emotion can be overwhelming. Therefore, the purposes of this chapter are to provide an outline of the nature of the events which take place after a child has died and to offer some indications of the aspects of care which need to be considered. The material provided is not intended to be exhaustive and should be taken in that context. However, the further reading list at the end of the chapter will suggest other sources of information on this very sensitive subject.

Legal aspects following a child's death

In some situations following the death of a child, the coroner must be informed. Such circumstances include the following where:

- there has been a sudden or unexpected death

- the circumstances of death are suspicious or there is evidence of violence

- death occurs within 24 hours of admission to hospital

- the deceased has had surgery within the last 6 months

- the deceased was not seen by a doctor within the 14 days prior to death

- the cause of death is unknown

- the deceased is a foster child, or has been in police or prison custody prior to death

- there is evidence of death having been related to industrial disease.

When any of these conditions apply to the child who has died, the doctor and coroner will discuss the case. Where the coroner believes there is sufficient cause for further inquiry into the circumstances surrounding death, a post-mortem will be ordered. In the case of the death of a child, the pathologist who undertakes this procedure should be a paediatric specialist (Clothier Report, 1993). The results of this post-mortem will form the coroner's decision about whether or not to open an inquest about the death. If the coroner decides that there are no grounds for intervention then the relevant certificates and documentation can be issued to the family and the child's body released so that the funeral can take place. Alternatively, the hospital at which the child died can request permission from the child's family to undertake a post-mortem to determine the cause of death, although this cannot go ahead without their consent. However, consent is not needed where the coroner orders the post-mortem and the family have no right to stop it proceeding even when this is in conflict with religious beliefs (Dimond, 1995).

If, following the results of the post-mortem, the coroner decides that an inquest into the death of the child is needed, it is always undertaken with the purpose of distinguishing one or all of the following:

- the identity of the deceased
- the circumstances of how, where and when death occurred
- to enable all the details currently required for registration of the death to become known.

(Dimond, 1995).

To accomplish this, the coroner will invite all the people involved with child's treatment at the time of death to make a statement about the circumstances in order to establish the facts of the situation. This also gives the family the opportunity to ask relevant questions where there may be evidence to support a claim for negligence. It is important to remember that the Coroner's Court in this country is not empowered to assign blame for the death of the child, and is for inquisitorial purposes only (Dimond, 1995). However, in some cases of public concern, the coroner can summon a jury who will, after hearing the evidence presented and under the direction of the coroner, offer a verdict on the cause of death which will be officially recorded.

The nature of emotional responses

While the legal aspects of the death of a child may be easily defined, the emotional consequences are much more difficult to either quantify or express. Wright (1996) suggests that the emotions involved in the death of a child can be related to the unnatural order of a child predeceasing older members of the family. Raphael (1984) goes further, suggesting that the death of a child is not expected in Western society and, where death is sudden, there is no time for preparative, anticipatory grief. As a consequence, the sudden death of a child equates with the highest intensity of bereavement and has the widest possible range of responses to it. Parkes (1975) additionally indicates that this type of bereavement has the most serious implications for difficulties in the recovery process which can be protracted. Therefore, it is important that when these situations arise, nursing staff respond to the situation appropriately and sensitively because of the far-reaching implications that poorly considered, immediate responses to this kind of situation can have (Wright, 1996). In practice, this means instigating actions which are in keeping with the family's wishes, as well as their cultural and religious beliefs. To do this effectively, Walsh and McGoldrick (1991) state that the impact of death on the family must be understood in the following terms:

- the nature of the prescribed rituals associated with dying, death and bereavement
- the nature of beliefs about the future where these exist for the deceased

- the nature of acceptable emotional responses to death as well as the way in which loss through death is integrated into life experience
- the nature of the role which gender plays in bereavement
- the nature of the stigmatisation which is afforded certain kinds of death and which are likely to be the most traumatic for the family.

In conjunction with the consideration given to these aspects, nurses must also accept that there are likely to be a whole range of possible emotional responses to the sudden death of a child some of which are very intense and uncomfortable to deal with. The purposes of these responses, demonstrated in the instinctive, physiological and psychological reactions of individuals, are to begin the process of adaptation to the loss and return to a different, but healthy and functional lifestyle without the person who has died (Marks, 1988). In making this adaptation, Worden (1983) highlights that there are four key tasks:

1. Accepting the reality of the loss.

2. Experiencing the pain of grief.

3. Adjusting to an environment in which the deceased is missing.

4. Withdrawing emotional energy and investing this in other relationships.

Success in dealing with these tasks, is often determined by factors which existed prior to the death such as the relationship with the deceased and the mode of death as well as characteristics of the person such as age, gender, personality and cultural and religious factors (Parkes, 1975). After death, subsequent social support, concurrent stresses and other life opportunities become important (Parkes, 1975). What is also clear is that responses to the family by health care professionals at the time of death are very important. In his survey of nurses who had had dealings with the suddenly bereaved, Wright (1996) found that there were nine common reactions by family members which nurses found particularly difficult to deal with. These were: withdrawal; denial; anger; isolation; bargaining; inappropriate responses; guilt; crying, sobbing and weeping, and acceptance. Some of these reactions are discussed, together with an indication of the ways in which nurses responses are felt to be useful by the bereaved.

Withdrawal

Wright (1996) describes this state as being where the bereaved person becomes quiet, inaccessible and mute. This state is particularly difficult for nurses because of the long periods of silence which accompany withdrawal and the lack of perceived value attached to 'being with' someone recently bereaved (Wright, 1996). In addition, there is a difficulty for nurses in that they often feel that nothing can be done physically to put things right which goes against many of the main premises of nursing. So, staying with the person is very difficult and the immediate reaction is quite understandably the need to leave the person alone. In contrast to nurses' beliefs about the therapeutic benefits of remaining with the bereaved person, Wright (1996) reports that people who are bereaved actually value the fact that someone stays with them during this period of withdrawal, and that it can be very frightening if they are left alone.

Denial

Denial that the death of someone important has occurred is a quite normal and expected reaction to bereavement. Indeed, it serves as an effective coping mechanism in the immediate period following the death of someone close (Kubler-Ross, 1978). However, Wright (1996) reports that if verbal denial continues for more than five minutes, nurses become very uncomfortable with the bereaved persons' response. In truth, it may take a long time to accept that a death has occurred, although assimilation that the news is true occurs very quickly. However, in the initial period after the news is broken, it can be very difficult for nurses to confirm and reinforce to a parent that their child has died, especially when to do so causes obvious distress (Wright, 1996). Though such a task is onerous and difficult, the benefits of helping a person in this way are often apparent later in the bereavement process where the ways in which parents were helped to begin to come to terms with their grief takes on new significance.

Anger

Anger is also an emotion which, in these circumstances, can be very powerful and enduring. There are no limits or even predictors about what issues bereaved parents may be angry about, and they can range from doctors involved in their child's care to God. In Wright's (1996) work, it is reported that the single most difficult thing for nurses to understand is anger at the dead person. Brewis (1995) adds that this kind of anger is often found in association with avoidable events which subsequently contributed to the child's death. Wright (1996) suggests that in this particular situation where anger is mobilised as a bereavement response, it may be difficult for nurses to deal with because of the need to defend or act as advocate for those who are unable to do this for themselves. For the bereaved, anger is cited as being a useful way to release strong feelings which are an essential element of the bereavement process and can result in a lower incidence of severe depression and anxiety at a later stage.

Guilt

Of all the emotions associated with early bereavement, guilt is perhaps the most easily triggered. Bereaved parents may feel guilty about a wide range of aspects of their care for their child and, where they may feel that they could have done a better job, these feelings can become focal. Brewis (1995) describes this kind of guilt as 'illogical guilt' and suggests that parents can best be helped in this situation by gentle reminding of all the positive aspects of parenting they accomplished for the child. However, guilt may persist long into the bereavement process and in some cases can become maladaptive. In some cases parents feel that they should have been the ones to die, or because of an action, for which they as parents were responsible, that they may have contributed to the cause of death. As life returns to a more usual routine, parents often feel guilty about laughing or finding enjoyment in every day activities (Brewis, 1995).

Helping parents

Helping parents to deal with their emotions following the death of their child is a very difficult task to accomplish. There are a wide variety of emotions which can be demonstrated by parents, although their expression will depend entirely on the person, their respective personality and background. As a result it can be difficult to know how to respond appropriately and what to say when confronted by bereaved parents. Brewis (1995) recognises this fact and suggests that nurses often try to say something they feel would be helpful in the situation instead of being ready to listen to how parents feel about their loss. In doing this however, Brewis (1995) cautions that there are some statements which quite clearly should be avoided by both health care professionals and friends of the bereaved. Brewis (1995) highlights examples of inappropriate statements that have been made to parents whose child recently died . These include:

I know how you feel.

You can always have another child.

Never mind its for the best.

More appropriate, are questions which give bereaved parents the opportunity to decide whether or not they wish to discuss the death of their child and to choose the right time and person with whom to disclose their feelings.

Other family members

Parents also need help to tell other children in the family about the death of their sibling. This can be a very difficult and painful experience for parents. There are several useful books available which help families to broach the subject of death together with their children, and to explore the feelings that a death within the family can evoke (see further reading list). Siblings have special problems in coping with death and in particular these can be related to the thought that they may have done something wrong or that the death of their brother or sister is a punishment for some previous misdemeanour. In response to such acute stress, children's behaviour can change and is usually observed as regression to previous stages of development such as thumb-sucking or bed-wetting. This can be very challenging for parents who, while trying to support their living children, are struggling to come to terms with their loss.

Grandparents too, find the death of a child particularly traumatic. In these unique circumstances grandparents find themselves grieving not only for the loss of their grandchild, but also for their own child whose pain they cannot ameliorate. Grandparents are especially susceptible to feeling guilty that they are still alive whilst their grandchild is dead. This is because grandparents often feel that they have had a long enough life compared to the short life of their grandchild.

Summary

When a child dies, life for the family who remain will never be the same again because the implications of bereavement are long-term and far-reaching. Helping families in the immediate aftermath of a sudden death requires nurses to respond appropriately and with sensitivity to the circumstances in which the family will find itself. This is because the approach taken by nurses involved with family at the time of the death of their child has the potential to affect the bereavement process far into the future. Therefore, nurses are in the unique position of being able to offer support and referral to other agencies where necessary which will help the family to begin to cope with their loss and adjust to a life without their child.

References

Brewis E (1995) Issues in Bereavement: There are no rules *Paediatr Nurs* **7**(9): 19–22

Dimond B (1995) *Legal Aspects of Nursing* 2nd Edition. Prentice Hall, London

Kubler-Ross E (1978) *To Live Until We Say Goodbye*. Prentice Hall, New Jersey

Marks M (1988) Death, dying bereavement and loss. In: Tiffany R, Webb P eds. *Oncology for Nurses Health Care Professional* 2nd Edition *Volume 2: Care and Support*. Harper and Row, Beaconsfield

Parkes CM (1975) Determinants of outcome following bereavement *Omega* **6**(4): 303–23

Raphael B (1984) *The Anatomy of Bereavement*. Hutchinson, London

Royal College of Surgeons (1992) *Guidelines for Daycase Surgery*. Royal College of Surgeons, London

Walsh F, McGoldrick (1991) *Living Beyond Loss: Death in the Family*. WW Norton, New York

Worden JW (1983) *Grief Counselling and Grief Therapy*. Tavistock Publications, London

Wright B (1996) *Sudden Death: A Research Base for Practice*. Churchill Livingstone, Edinburgh

Further reading

The books and articles listed below are a useful variety of materials which cover different perspectives on the death of a child. Some are research-based, providing valuable insights. While others are specifically written to help nurses, families and other relatives discuss death with children.

Bluebond-Langer M (1978) *The Private World of Dying Children*. Princeton Press, New Jersey

Heegaard ME (1988) *When Someone Very Special Dies*. Woodlan Press, New York

Judd D (1989) *Give Sorrow Words — Working with Dying Children*. Free Association Books, London

Kubkler-Ross E (1983) *On Children and Death*. MacMillan, New York

Mackay LH (1995) Perioperative deaths of children. *Br J Theatre Nurs* 4(12): 12–14

Stickney D (1982) *Water Bugs and Dragonflies — Explaining Death to Children*. Mowbray, London

9

Planning care for children having surgery

Key issues and concepts

- The purpose of planning care and documentation

- Recommendations for record keeping

- Using the nursing process and models to guide the planning of care

---

The purpose of planning care and documentation

Legally, the need for, and power of planning care in the form of documentation is increasing and the accurate recording of events has become ever more important in recent years (Edelstein, 1990). In addition, consumer oriented philosophies of health care delivery have heightened the need for effective documentation, particularly in terms of accountability for nursing actions (Walton, 1986; Department of Health, 1991). Indeed, the Health Service Ombudsman's Report underlines the importance of keeping detailed records as evidence that care has actually been given (Walton, 1986). However, Gropper (1988) reports that many nurses view documentation as a chore which reduces their contact time with the patient and their families. Hence, there is poor compliance with the standards laid down by statutory bodies. Unfortunately, nurses fail to realise the importance of documentary evidence of care given until they are required to appear in court. As a result, standards for records and record keeping have been produced by the United Kingdom Central Council for Nursing, Midwifery and Health Visiting (UKCC). In this advisory document, the UKCC confirm that making and keeping records is an essential part of the whole process of nursing (UKCC, 1993). Further, the Council reminds nurses that failure to keep accurate records could result in the contravention of at least two clauses of the *Code of Professional Conduct* (UKCC, 1992). The UKCC (1993) states that the purposes of record keeping is to:

1. Provide accurate, current, comprehensive and concise information concerning the patient or client and associated observations.

2. Provide a record of any problems that arise and the action taken in response to them.

3. Provide evidence of care required, intervention by professional practitioners and patient or client responses.

4. Include a record of any factors (physical, psychological or social) that appear to affect the patient or client.

5. Record the chronology of events and the reasons for decisions made.

6. Support standard setting, quality assessment and audit.

7. Provide a baseline against which improvement or deterioration may be judged.

In order to document care effectively Fischbach (1991) suggests that nurses need to be confident in their written communication skills, documentation of the nursing process and the ways in which they adhere to standards of documentation laid down nationally and locally. These skills cannot be developed overnight, so it is important that sufficient practice is gained during nurse training together with an assimilation of the ways in which documentation relates to the process of planning care itself. Hunt and Marks-Maran (1980) defined the process as:

A systematic approach to planning patient care which enables the nurse to provide effective nursing which will meet the individual needs of the patient.

A nursing care plan constitutes the,

...visible and written record of the implementation of care planning. It documents the use of this approach and has the following features:

- *a nursing assessment of the patient*
- *details of the care planned to meet the patient's problems and needs (both during admission and on discharge)*
- *evaluation of the care given.*

(Hunt and Marks-Maran, 1980, p 6)

Transferring these details into practical documentation of care given often takes the form of a model of nursing. Underpinning a model of nursing there is a philosophy about the way in which the person receiving care is perceived and a framework with which to examine events from a global perspective. Common to all models of nursing are four parameters of consideration:

1.   The person receiving the nursing.

2.   The environment in which the person exists.

3.   The health-illness state of the person.

4.   Nursing actions.

(Field, 1987).

What changes from model to model is the style in which the information is gathered and presented as a care plan for example, in Roper, Logan and Tierney's (1985) Activities of Living Model, the focus surrounds the ability of the person to perform the suggested activities for themselves along a dependence-independence continuum which is dependent upon the person's place in their lifespan. In Orem's (1985) model the focus is on self-care activities whereas Roy (1976) views adaptation as the pivotal issue. However, in practice there are often difficulties in application because some nurses believe that nursing is a collection of tasks designed to assist the implementation of medical care. As a result, the underpinning values and philosophies of the model authors and the relationship between the assessment and development of a care plan are confused (McKenna, 1990; Field, 1987). Other factors such as the length of hospital stay, ward resources and staffing levels can also impinge on the reasons why nurses do not use models of nursing to guide care planning adequately. However, it is clear that using a model of nursing to guide the assessment, planning and delivery of care has significant benefits for the patient and nurse in terms of communication of essential aspects of care; the development of knowledge about the child and their family; documentation of progress towards stated goals of care, and as a teaching tool within the ward environment.

The process of care planning for the child is not a concept which is difficult to understand. Essentially, there are four distinct stages: Assessment; Planning; Implementation and Evaluation with each stage informing the next. The type of information gathered and prepared at each stage is pertinent to the model in use, although the ways in which this information is used to prepare a care plan can be significantly different from model to model, as indeed can the format of documentation devised to accompany the model of nursing. Perhaps one of the easiest ways of understanding how each stage relates to the next and the way in which the nursing process can be guided by models of nursing and applied to practice is to use a case study example which follows a child and their family through the surgical experience, drawing together the importance of pre- and post-operative aspects of care discussed in *Chapters 2, 3* and *4*.

Case history

Neil is 6 years old. Over the past eighteen months, he has suffered from recurrent sore throats which have been treated with antibiotics from his general practitioner (GP). As a result of these illnesses, Neil has missed a substantial amount of his first year at school. Therefore, Neil's GP. referred him to the children's ear, nose and throat (ENT) specialist at the nearby hospital. Following this consultation, Neil and his mum were told that surgery would be required to remove his tonsils and adenoids. This was booked as an elective admission six weeks from the initial consultation with the ENT specialist. Neil's mum was advised that there would be an opportunity for her to bring Neil to the pre-admission clinic on the Saturday morning immediately before the date of the planned surgery. She was also told that attendance at this clinic would offer the opportunity for Neil to start the process of preparation for his admission and to undergo an initial medical and nursing assessment prior to admission.

In the intervening weeks, Neil's mum talked to him about his forthcoming admission, carefully explaining what she knew about the reasons for the operation and the length of time it had been anticipated that Neil would be in hospital. On the Saturday before the date of the planned admission, Neil and his mum went to the pre-admission clinic.

Pre-admission visits

The value and purpose of children attending pre-admission visits to the hospital is explained at length in *Chapters 1* and *2*. However, these visits also give nursing staff the opportunity to begin the process of planning care for the child and his/her family. At such visits, it is possible to instigate the beginnings of history taking and assessment, documenting findings which can be completed on admission to the ward. *Figure 9.1* provides an example of the kind of history taking which was completed on Neil's pre-admission visit.

Figure 9.1: History sheet (adapted from Smith, 1995)

Child's name: Surname: *Holden* First name: *Neil* Likes to be called: *Neil*	**Registration number:** *158973KB*	**Date of admission:**	**Consultant:** *Godfrey*
	Ward: *Penguin*	**Time:**	**Child's nurse:** **Team:**
Address: *4 Ashfield* *Bourton* *Fellenshire* **Telephone number:** *78102*	**Age:** *6yrs 6mths* **Date of birth:** *05:05:91* **Religion:** *Church of England*	**Reason for this admission:** *Removal of tonsils and adenoids*	**Reasons for previous admission:** *No previous admission* **Medical history of note:** *Recurrent sore throats over last 18mths requiring antibiotic therapy from GP*
Next of kin: *Nancy Holden* **Address:** *4 Ashfield* *Bourton* *Fellenshire* **Telephone Numbers** **Work:** *76706* **Home:** *78102* **Relationship to child:** *Mother*	**Social circumstances:** *Maternal grandparents are looking after Neil's siblings for the duration of admission. Will only visit if admission is longer than one night. Dad will visit after work. Mum has taken time off work to stay with Neil until he is ready to return to school*	**Child's understanding of reason for this admission:** *To make sore throat get better so he can go back to school*	**Will anyone be resident with the child:** ~~Yes~~/~~No~~ **Where:** **Name:**
Who does the child live with: *Mum, Dad and siblings*	**Names and ages of brothers and sisters:** *Ffion aged 11yrs/Dean aged 8yrs*	**Parents' understanding of reason for admission:** *Removal of tonsils and adenoids*	**Medical diagnosis:** *Admitted for adenotonsillectomy*
Who has parental responsibility: *Parents*			

Allergies: *None known*	**General practioner:** *Dr.Goldsmith*
Recent contact with any infectious diseases: *None known*	**Address:** *The Practice, High St, Bourton*
Current medication: *None being taken*	**Telephone:** *79456*
Height: *124cm* **Weight:** *22kg*	**Health visitor** **Address:** *Not applicable*
Immunisation history: *All immunisations up to date to time of pre-school booster*	**Telephone:**
Other information relevant to admission: *Neil and his mum attended pre-admission on 30th October 1997 (A.S.Glover 30/10/97)*	**Other contacts (with names and address):** *School Nurse Mrs Dempsey The Practice, High St, Bourton*

Parent facilities:
Fire regulations
Ward contact number given
Shower/toilet facilities
Parent's kitchen
Ward kitchen
Dining room facilities

Discharge checklist:
Parent(s)/child informed of planned discharge date:
Parent(s)/child agree discharge appropriate:
Discharge advice sheet given and explained:
Necessary teaching completed:
Equipment on loan:
Outpatient appointment given:
Medicines given:
Own medicines returned:
GP letter given:
Health visitor/other health care contacts informed:
Ward contact telephone number given:
Discharge completed by:
Date:

Signature of nurse taken history: *A.S.Glover*
Date: *30/10/97*

Signature of ward nurse:
Date:

History taking

History taking is usually the starting point from which nurses can begin to develop an individualised plan of care for the child and their family. Therefore, the kinds of details that are gathered during history taking are related to the particular circumstances of the child and his/her family. For example, the social situation of the family which may have implications for gaining consent for surgery; the kinds of previous admissions and prior experience of hospitalisation which can affect the type of explanation the child is given. It is important to discover what the child understands about the nature and purpose of admission so that similar terms can be used by nursing staff to those already used by the child's family. Details should be taken about community health care professionals who may be involved with the child and the family so that appropriate communication and liaison can take place when considering discharge planning. Smith (1995) also suggests that involving the family from the outset in developing care activities has the benefits of ensuring that the partnership between nurses and the family is explicit from the outset and maximises the amount of in-depth information that can be gathered from the people who know the child best.

Admission to the ward

On admission to the ward, the accuracy of the details gathered in the pre-admission clinic needs to be checked and the nurse completing the remainder of the history sheet should also verify that there are no other details which need to be added to the original history. *Figure 9.2* is an example of the way in which the remaining details can be completed.

Figure 9.2: Completed history sheet (adapted from Smith, 1995)

Child's name: Surname: *Holden* First name: *Neil* Likes to be called: *Neil*	**Registration number:** *158973KB*	**Date of admission:** *4/11/97*	**Consultant:** *Godfrey*
Address: *4 Ashfield Bourton Fellenshire* Telephone number: *78102*	**Ward:** *Penguin* **Age:** *6yrs 6mths* **Date of birth:** *05:05:91* **Religion:** *Church of England*	**Time:** *0800 hours* **Reason for this admission:** *Removal of tonsils and adenoids*	**Child's nurse:** *Frances Marks* **Team:** *Duck* **Reasons for previous admission:** *No previous admission* **Medical history of note:** *Recurrent sore throats over last 18mths requiring antibiotic therapy from GP*
Next of kin: *Nancy Holden* **Address:** *4 Ashfield Bourton Fellenshire* **Telephone Numbers** **Work:** *76706* **Home:** *78102* **Relationship to child:** *Mother*	**Social circumstances:** *Maternal grandparents are looking after Neil's siblings for the duration of admission. Will only visit if admission is longer than one night. Dad will visit after work. Mum has taken time off work to stay with Neil until he is ready to return to school*	**Child's understanding of reason for this admission:** *To make sore throat get better so he can go back to school*	**Will anyone be resident with the child:** ~~Yes~~/~~No~~ **Where:** *By Neil's bed* **Name:** *Nancy Holden*
Who does the child live with: *Mum, Dad and siblings* **Who has parental responsibility:** *Parents*	**Names and ages of brothers and sisters:** *Ffion aged 11yrs/Dean aged 8yrs*	**Parents' understanding of reason for admission:** *Removal of tonsils and adenoids*	**Medical diagnosis:** *Admitted for adenotonsillectomy*

Allergies: *None known*	**Parent facilities:** Fire regulations : *yes*	**General practioner:** *Dr.Goldsmith* **Address:** *The Practice, High St, Bourton* **Telephone:** *79456*
Recent contact with any infectious diseases: *None known*	Ward contact number given *yes*	**Health visitor Address:** *Not applicable*
Current medication: *None being taken*	Shower/toilet facilities: **yes** Parent's kitchen: **yes** Ward kitchen: **yes**	**Telephone:**
Height: *124cm* **Weight:** *22kg*	Dining room facilities: *yes*	**Other contacts (with names and address):** *School Nurse Mrs Dempsey The Practice, High St, Bourton*

Discharge checklist:
Parent(s)/child informed of planned discharge date:
Parent(s)/child agree discharge appropriate:
Discharge advice sheet given and explained:
Necessary teaching completed:
Equipment on loan:
Outpatient appointment given:
Medicines given:
Own medicines returned:
GP letter given:
Health visitor/other health care contacts informed:
Ward contact telephone number given:
Discharge completed by:
Date:

Immunisation history:
All immunisations up to date to time of pre-school booster

Signature of nurse taken history: *A.S.Glover* **Date:** *30/10/97*

Other information relevant to admission:
Neil and his mum attended pre-admission on 30th October 1997 (A.S.Glover 30/10/97)
No other information gathered at admission to the ward. (F.J.Marks)

Signature of ward nurse: *F.J.Marks* **Date:** *4/11/97*

Assessment

The purpose of conducting an in-depth assessment of the child is to ascertain what the child's usual routine is, and how this might have changed because of the underlying condition which necessitated admission and ultimately, to provide the informational basis upon which care can be planned. In the example given in *Figure 9.3,* Neil's assessment is in 3 stages. In meeting the first objective, ascertaining usual routines, the admitting nurse completes the 'Usual level of activity' column. There is an assessment of daily activities using, in this case, Roper, Logan and Tierney's (1985) Activities of Living Assessment framework. On this part of the assessment it is possible to see that a whole range of aspects of Neil's usual pattern of behaviour have been assessed. This is done in order to provide a baseline against which changes can be judged, and so that as far as possible, Neil's usual routines can be mirrored during admission. In the second stage of the assessment, 'Pre-operative level of activity', the changes occurring as a result of admission and the underlying condition for which surgery is needed are documented. It is important to recognise that not all activities will be changed as a result of either the admission or illness and, in such cases, the nurse completing the assessment should clearly document this. This is for reasons of ease of communication to other members of staff and also to demonstrate that the aspect of living has been considered.

On the assessment sheet shown in *Figure 9.3* it is possible to see that many of the aspects discussed in relation to pre-operative care (see *Chapter 3*) have been reflected in the type of information that has been gathered for example, the baseline recordings of vital signs; the kind of pre-operative preparation which has been delivered prior to admission; the kinds of measures which Neil finds comforting during time of distress, and aspects of pre-operative teaching that have been employed such as instruction on the use of an appropriate pain assessment tool. The third stage of Neil's assessment is not actually made until he returns from theatre after surgery.

Figure 9.3: Pre-operative assessment sheet (adapted from Smith, 1995)

		Date of initial assessment: *4/11/97*	Signature of nurse making assessment: *F.J.Marks*
Child's name: *Neil Holden*	**Registration No:** *158973KB*		
Date of birth: *5th May 1991*	**Consultant:** *Godfrey*	**Time of initial assessment:** *0800 hours*	
Activity of living	**Usual level of activity**	**Pre-operative level of activity**	**Post-operative level of activity**
Breathing and circulation	*No breathing or circulation problems*	*Neil's breathing is regular with no noise. He is pink and shows no signs of respiratory distress. Rate 23/min. Pulse=100/min BP=105/60*	
Maintaining a safe environment	*Mum reports that Neil has no special difficulties maintaining his own safety*	*Neil has attended pre-admission clinic. He will need to be prepared for theatre using techniques described on care plan*	
Communicating	*Neil is usually an articulate child who has no difficulty communicating*	*Pre-operative teaching of pain assessment tool undertaken*	*Neil will use the faces rating scale in the post-operative period*
Play and education	*Neil has missed a lot of school during the past year because of his recurrent sore throats*	*No changes assessed*	*When he feels unwell, Mum says that he likes to watch videos and sit quietly*
Personal hygiene and dressing	*Neil usually washes and bathes himself and chooses his own clothes at the weekend, although he wears school uniform in the week*	*No changes assessed*	

Activity of living	Usual level of activity	Pre-operative level of activity	Post-operative level of activity
Controlling body temperature	*Neil suffers from high temperatures when he has a chest infection, but is not susceptible to febrile convulsions*	*Afebrile Temperature via the axillary route: 36.7°C*	
Mobilising	*Neil is usually very active. He rides his bike and loves to play football when he is at home*	*No change assessed*	
Sleeping	*Bedtime is at 7.00pm on schooldays. Neil likes his toy tiger to go to bed with at night*	*Toy tiger needs to accompany Neil to theatre to be used as a comforter following surgery*	
Eating and drinking	*Neil usually has a good appetite when his throat is not sore. He does not like Brussels sprouts or spinach. His favourite drink is cola*	*Neil is due to go to theatre at 1.30pm. He should be fasted from 10.30 am*	
Eliminating	*Neil does not usually have any problems eliminating*	*No changes assessed*	
Expressing sexuality	*Neil and his family have no strong religious beliefs. Neil gets embarrassed when girls are around and he needs to change clothes etc*	*No changes assed*	
Dying	*Neil does not really understand much about dying. He has had no recent bereavements that may worry him during admission.*	*Mum says that she is aware of the risks associated with the operation Neil is having but she has not discussed this with Neil*	

Figure 9.4: Post-operative assessment sheet (adapted from Smith, 1995)

Child's name: *Neil Holden*	Registration No: *158973KB*	Date of initial assessment: *4/11/97*	Signature of nurse making assessment: *F.J.Marks*
Date of birth: *5th May 1991*	**Consultant:** *Godfrey*	**Time of initial assessment:** *0800 hours*	
Activity of living	**Usual level of activity**	**Pre-operative level of activity**	**Post-operative level of activity**
Breathing and circulation	*No breathing or circulation problems*	*Neil's breathing is regular with no noise. He is pink and shows no signs of respiratory distress. Rate 23/min. Pulse=100/min. BP=105/60*	*No sign of respiratory distress=19/min No fresh bleeding from mouth or nose. Observation within normal limits on return from theatre pulse=105/min. BP 100/65*
Maintaining a safe environment	*Mum reports that Neil has no special difficulties maintaining his own safety*	*Neil has attended pre-admission clinic. He will need to be prepared for theatre using techniques described on the care plan*	*At risk of post-operative complications of haemorrhage shock*
Communicating	*Neil is usually an articulate child who has no difficulty communicating*	*Pre-operative pain assessment tool undertaken*	*Neil will use the faces rating scale in the post-operative period Pain tool used in theatre. Neil is not in teaching about pain on return to ward.*
Play and education	*Neil has missed a lot of school during the past year because of his recurrent sore throats*	*No changes assessed*	*When he feels unwell, Mum says that he likes to watch videos and sit quietly. Neil is asleep on return to ward*
Personal hygiene and dressing	*Neil usually washes and bathes himself and chooses his own clothes at the weekend, although he wears school uniform in the week*	*No changes assessed*	*No changes assessed*

Activity of living	Usual level of activity	Pre-operative level of activity	Post-operative level of activity
Controlling body temperature	Neil suffers from high temperatures when he has a chest infection, but is not susceptible to febrile convulsions	Afebrile temperature via the axillary route: 36.7°C	Auxillary temperature 36.3°C on return to ward
Mobilising	Neil is usually very active. He rides his bike and loves to play football when he is at home	No change assessed	Neil is asleep on return to the ward
Sleeping	Bedtime is at 7.00pm on schooldays. Neil likes his toy tiger to go to bed with at night	Toy tiger needs to accompany Neil to theatre to be used as a comforter following surgery	Toy tiger in use for comfort following surgery
Eating and drinking	Neil usually has a good appetite when his throat is not sore. He does not like Brussels sprouts or spinach. His favourite drink is cola	Neil is due to go to theatre at 1.30pm. He should be fasted from 10.30 am	Neil has not had anything to eat or drink since returning to the ward
Eliminating	Neil does not usually have any problems eliminating	No changes assessed	Has not passed urine since returning to the ward
Expressing sexuality	Neil and his family have no strong religious beliefs. Neil gets embarressed when girls are around and he needs to change clothes etc	No changes assed	No changes assessed
Dying	Neil does not really understand much about dying. He has had no recent bereavements that may worry him during admission.	Mum says that she is aware of the risks associated with the operation Neil is having but she has not discussed this with Neil	No changes assessed

However, it is possible to see in the assessment shown in *Figure 9.4* that additional information has been gathered about Neil's condition following surgery which can be compared against both usual and pre-operative behaviours. Once the assessment process is complete, care planning can begin.

Planning care

The main premise of planning care is that where a discrepancy between normal behaviour and that identified in association with admission or illness exists, an intervention is needed to assist the child to return wherever possible to their usual level of behaviour. However, this is probably an over-simplification of the circumstances of care planning because there are other things which need to considered which the assessment may not always reveal. For instance, there are activities which may not yet be affected by admission or illness, but that could be affected during the course of the admission or by the illness and its treatment. These types of problems are often referred to as 'potential problems' and also require consideration during the planning phase of the process. Therefore, assimilation of actual and potential problems requires the children's nurse to have a great deal of understanding about the procedure for which the child has been admitted and the potential impact this may have on both the child and the family, physically, psychologically and socially, so that the process of prioritising those aspects of care which need attention and suggestions for the ways that this can be accomplished begins. A useful way to consider that all such aspects of care planning are addressed is to use the Davies and Klein's (1994) framework in collaboration with the model of nursing in use (see *Chapters 3* and *4* for indications of the types of issues which can be considered at this stage of care planning).

From the assessment in *Figure 9.3* and the care plan shown in *Figure 9.5*, it is clear that the only change as a result of admission for surgery stems from the fact that Neil needs to be safely prepared for his general anaesthetic.

Figure 9.5: Pre-operative care plan

Name: *Neil* *Holden*	Registration No: *158973KB*	Ward: *Penguin*	Consultant: *Godfrey*

Activity of living:
Maintaining a safe environment

Problem identified:
Neil is at risk of compromise to his safety, physical and psychological, during the pre-operative stage

Goal statement:
1. Neil will be safely physically prepared for theatre using the pre-operative checklist

2. Neil will have all pre-operative procedures explained in relevant terms in order to maintain his psychological safety

Date	Nursing action	Sign
4/11/97 *0845hrs*	• *Instigate the use of the pre-operative checklist completing all details relevant to Neil's care prior to transfer to theatre* • *Explain to Neil all procedures using words and phrases with which he is familiar* • *Administer pre-operative medication as prescribed* • *Explain to Mum what she will see when Neil is taken to theatre*	 *F.J. Marks* *Staff Nurse*

Date	Family actions	Sign
4/11/97 *0845hrs*	• *Mum wishes to accompany Neil into the anaesthetic room* • *Mum will make sure that Neil has nothing to eat or drink after 10.30am* • *Mum will make sure that pre-cannulation cream is undisturbed prior to theatre*	 *F.J. Marks* *Staff Nurse* *NHHolden*

Figure 9.5: Pre-operative care plan continued (theatre check list)

Personal information

Child's name: *Neil Holden*	HospitalNo:*158973KB*	Ward: *Penguin*
Likes to be called: *Neil*	Consultant: *Godfrey*	
Address: *4 Ashfield*	Proposed operation: *Adenotonsillectomy*	
Bourton Fellenshire	Allergies: *None known*	

Pre-operative physical assessment

Pre-operative observations:

Temperature	Pulse	Respiration	B/P	Cuff size	Limb
36.7°C	*110/min*	*23/min*	*105*	*3*	*right*
		-	*60*		*arm*

Weight	Height	Urinalysis	Sickle cell result
22kg	*124cm*	*No abnormalities*	*N/A*

Checklist

Identification braclet checked	Y	N̶	
Consent form signed	Y	N̶	
Pre-medication given	Y̶	N̶	NA
Pre-cannulation cream applied

Site: Backs of right and left hands | Y | N̶ | N̶A̶ |
| Fasted
Time of last drink:10.30am

Time of last food: 7.00am | Y | N̶ | |
| Jewellery removed/made safe

Site: | Y̶ | N̶ | NA |
Make up/nail varnish removed	Y̶	N̶	NA
Prosthesis/contact lenses removed	Y̶	N̶	NA
Braces removed	Y̶	N̶	NA
Loose teeth/caps/crowns

Site: | Y̶ | N | N̶A̶ |

Equipment in situ pre-operatively

None	Site:
	Site:
	Site:
	Site:
	Site:

Figure 9.5: Pre-operative care plan(continued)		
Accompanying child to theatre		
Case note	Y	N̶
X-rays	Y̶	N
Toy/comforter: *Toy tiger* Describe: *soft furry toy*	Y	N̶
Parent Explanation: *Given on the ward by nursing staff*	Y	N̶

Child's individual needs:	
Special instruction: *Neil is able to use the faces rating scale to assess pain*	Preparation for high dependency following surgery *N/A*
Child would like sutures/plasters following surgery *N/A*	Special words used by child: *'HURT' for pain*
Other needs: *Mum is available to come to recovery following Neil's operation*	Other needs: *None assessed*
Ward Nurse signature: *F.J.Marks* Date: *4/11/97* Time: *11.00am*	Theatre staff signature: Date: Time:

Therefore, the care plan produced reflects this in the statement of the pre-operative problem and the aim of care is explained in the form of two, measurable goal statements. Appropriate interventions are then described which relate to both the assessment of the child's circumstances achieved earlier in the process and the additional knowledge which is available to the children's nurse because of her understanding of the requirements of children and their families during the pre-operative period ie. the research base, rationale and other evidence which suggests that such actions are appropriate for the child and their family. Similarly, once the post-operative assessment is carried out following surgical intervention, care can subsequently be planned for this period using similar principles (see *Figures 9.6–9.11*). Other aspects of planning care which need to be considered are the ways in which family members want to be involved in delivering the care their child and this should be documented within the care plan as demonstrated in each of the samples.

Evaluating the implementation of planned care

Evaluating care is an ongoing process which leads to refinement of existing problems and resolving of those which are no longer issues for the child or their family. This is usually achieved by a written record which serves the double purpose of being a useful communication tool between members of nursing staff and allied health care professionals as well as serving as a permanent record of care in conjunction with the assessment sheets and care plans produced. Evaluation statements within the care plan need not be lengthy or verbose volumes. Succinct, accurate records are key and these need to give an up-to-date and informative account of progress towards goals of care. Where progress is not achieved, the record should include reasons why no progress could be made and the type of remedial action to be considered. Such re-assessment may necessitate the re-writing of some problems, goals and nursing actions in order to account for changes identified. A sample evaluation of Neil's care plan is shown in *Figure 9.12*.

Figure 9.6: Post-operative care plan (a)

Name: Neil Holden	Registration No: 158973KB	Ward: Penguin	Consultant: Godfrey

Activity of living:
Breathing and circulation

Problem identified:
Neil is at risk of airway obstruction, haemorrhage and shock following surgical intervention to remove his tonsils and adenoids

Goal statement:
1. Signs of any post-operative complications will be monitored for the post-operative phase of the procedure

2. Any complications detected through careful monitoring will be reported to medical staff

Date	Nursing actions	Sign
4/11/97 1545 hrs	• *Monitor Neil's pulse and blood pressure every half hour until they have remained within the usual limits for 2 hours. Repeat this process, decreasing the frequency between each set of observations as they remain stable. Repeat this cycle until observations are completed every 4 hours. A rise in pulse rate and decrease in blood pressure should be reported immediately because it is a sign of shock or haemorrhage* • *Observe Neil's mouth and nose for signs of fresh bleeding. Check pillowcase for drainage from mouth while asleep* • *Observe for signs of excessive swallowing which can indicate blood loss at the back of the throat. Report such findings to medical staff immediately* • *Observe and record Neil's respritory rate and effort. Check for unusual noises during inspiration and expiration. Note colour of extremities and lips* • *Oxygen and suction apparatus will be beside Neil's bed as a matter of precaution*	*F.J.Marks Staff Nurse*

Date	Family actions	Sign
4/11/97 1545 hrs	• *Neil's Mum will alert nursing staff if she is worried about his condition in between recording his observations* • *The purpose of all equipment and routine post-operative care will be explained to Neil's mum so that she is not unduly worried*	*F.J.Marks Staff Nurse NHHolden*

Figure 9.7: Post-operative care plan (b)			

Name: *Neil Holden*	**Registration No:** *158973KB*	**Ward:** *Penguin*	**Consultant:** *Godfrey*

Activity of living:
Maintaining a safe environment

Problem identified:
Neil is at risk of compromise to his safety, physical and psychological, during the post-operative period

Goal statement:
1. Neil's safety will be maintained during the post-operative period culminating in a safe recovery from his general anaesthetic

Date	Nursing actions	Sign
4/11/97 1545hrs	• *Post-operative complications will be monitored for using the care plan devised for breathing and circulation* • *Until Neil is fully recovered from the anaesthetic he will be closely observed to prevent him injuring himself* • *Nurses or mum will accompany Neil to the toilet until he is fully recovered from the general anaesthetic* • *Neil's bedspace will be kept free from unused or unneeded equipment to prevent injury by tripping or falling*	*F.J.Marks Staff Nurse*

Date	Family actions	Sign
4/11/97 1545hrs	• *Mum will stay with Neil in the immediate post-operative period until he is fully awake following anaesthetic* • *Mum will tell nursing staff when she is leaving Neil, however briefly, so that he is closely observed at all times* • *Mum will accompany Neil to the toilet if he needs this facility until he has recovered from the anaesthetic*	*F.J.Marks Staff Nurse* NHHolden

Figure 9.8: Post-operative care plan (c)

Name: *Neil* *Holden*	Registration No: *158973KB*	Ward: *Penguin*		Consultant: *Godfrey*

Activity of living:
Communicating

Problem identified:
Neil has had his tonsils and adenoids removed which is a painful procedure in the post-operative phase. Therefore, Neil needs to be able to communicate about his pain to members of nursing staff so that it can be controlled

Goal statement:
Using the Faces Pain Assessment Tool, Neil will be able to communicate with nursing staff about the intensity of his pain following surgical intervention

Date	Nursing actions	Sign
4/11/97 *1545 hrs*	• *Neil has been introduced to the Faces Pain Assessment Tool in the pre-operative period and is familiar with its use. Therefore, nursing staff must use only this tool in the post-operative period* • *Administer analgesia as prescribed* • *Assess Neil's pain 20 minutes following administration of a dose of analgesia to determine its effect* • *Continue to monitor Neil's pain behaviour in between doses of analgesia for non-verbal signs of pain. Where such behaviour exsists use the assessment tool to determine severity and adminsister alternative forms of analgesia prescribed. Monitor the effectiveness of the doses as before*	*F.J.Marks* *Staff Nurse*

Date	Family actions	Sign
4/11/97 *1545hrs*	• *Mum will inform nursing staff if she feels that Neil is in pain between doses of analegesia* • *Mum will assist nursing staff in making an assessment of Neil's pain using the Faces Assesssment tool* • *Mum will assist nursing staff to administer analgesia prescribed*	*F.J.Marks* *Staff Nurse* *NHHolden*

Figure 9.9: Post-operative care plan (d)			
Name: *Neil* *Holden*	**Registration No:** *158973KB*	**Ward:** *Penguin*	**Consultant**: *Godfrey*

Activity of living:
Controlling body temperature

Problem identified:
Neil is at risk of developing an infection at the site of his tonsil beds 48–72 hours following surgey

Goal statement:
1. *To instigate measures which will reduce the risk of Neil's developing an infection*
2. *To explain to mum what she should observe Neil for when she takes him home since Neil will have been discharged from hospital during the critical period*

Date	Nursing actions	Sign
4/11/97 *1545 hrs*	• *Encourage Neil to begin eating and drinking ordinary family foods as soon as possible following surgery to prevent the development of slough at the tonsil beds which may predipose him to the development of infection* • *Plan time to spend with Neil's mum to explain about when and how to take Neil's temperature when he is discharged from hospital* • *Explain to Neil's mum about the signs and symtoms of infection following tonsillectomy* • *Give mum a copy of the post-operative instructions to read prior to discharge* • *Plan time to answer any questions mum may have in relation to this information*	*F.J.Marks* *Staff Nurse*
Date	**Family actions**	**Sign**
4/11/97 *1545 hrs*	• *Mum will read post-operative care discharge instructions before leaving the ward* • *Mum knows that she can ask any questions she may have at the time* • *Mum will encourage Neil to eat and drink normally as soon as he has recovered from the anaesthetic*	*F.J.Marks* *Staff Nurse* *NHHolden*

Figure 9.10: Post-operative care plan (e)			
Name: *Neil Holden*	**Registration No:** *158973KB*	**Ward:** *Penguin*	**Consultant**: *Godfrey*

Activity of living:
Eating and drinking

Problem identified:
Neil needs to begin eating and drinking normal family foods as soon as possible after recovery from his anaesthetic to prevent the development of slough at the tonsil beds

Goal statement:
Neil will be able to eat and drink normal family foods within 24hrs of his recovery from anaesthetic

Date	Nursing actions	Sign
4/11/97 1545 hrs	• *Ensure that Neil has sufficient analgesia before encouraging him to eat and drink in the immediate post-operative period* • *Use the Pain Assessment tool to ensure that Neil is pain free prior to mealtimes* • *Begin the reintroduction of food and drink by offering Neil small amounts of water/orange juice and gradually increase this* • *Encourage Neil to eat ordinary foods rather than soft, easily swallable foods, to prevent the build up of slough on the tonsil beds*	*F.J.Marks Staff Nurse*

Date	Family actions	Sign
4/11/97 1545hrs	• *Mum will encourage Neil to eat and drink normally in the post-operative period* • *Mum will provide Neil's favourite type of orange juice to offer when he has recovered from his anaesthetic*	*F.J.Marks Staff Nurse NHHolden*

Figure 9.11: Post-operative care plan (f)

Name: *Neil* *Holden*	Registration No: *158973KB*	Ward: *Penguin*	Consultant: *Godfrey*

Activity of living:
Eliminating

Problem identified:
Neil is at risk of urinary retention following anaesthesia

Goal statement:
Neil will pass urine within 18 hours of his return from theatre

Date	Nursing actions	Sign
4/11/97 *1545 hrs*	• *Monitor Neil's urinary output until he passes urine in the period following surgery* • *Observe Neil for any signs of abdominal discomfort which may indicate an overfull bladder* • *Maintain Neil's privacy and dignity if he needs to use a urine bottle on the ward* • *Report lack of urine output to medical staff tomorrw morning if Neil has not passed urine by then. This is because his normal bedtime is 7.00pm and then he usually sleeps through the night*	*F.J.Marks* *Staff Nurse*

Date	Family actions	Sign
4/11/97 *1545hrs*	• *Mum will let nursing staff know when Neil passes urine* • *Mum will assist Neil to use a urine bottle if this is necessary*	*F.J.Marks* *Staff Nurse* *NHHolden*

Figure 9.12: Evaluation notes

Time	Evaluation	Sign
0845 hrs	*Neil and his mum were admitted to the ward this morning. Doctors informed of his arrival. Neil is being physically prepared for theatre using the pre-operative check list. He is aware of all the interventions that will be made this morning. No oral pre-medication is to be prescribed. Pre-cannulation cream to be put on at 12.30pm Mum has been told about accompanying Neil to theatre. She would like to stay with Neil while he is induced. Neil and his mum understand that he must have nothing to eat or drink from 10.30am*	*F.J.Marks* *Staff Nurse*
1545 hrs	*Arrived back on the ward following planned adenotonsillectomy. Post-operative assessment undertaken and care planned. Neil's condition is stable on return to ward. He is a little sleepy. He has not had a drink or passed urine since waking up from his anaesthetic. The last dose of analgesia was administered in theatre.*	*F.J.Marks* *Staff Nurse*

Summary

Operationalising care planning skills can be difficult to master initially. However, it is clear that for legal and professional reasons it is something which needs to be accomplished. care planning and the delivery of care actions identified is the culmination of a great deal of knowledge surrounding caring for children having surgery and their families. To do this effectively, children's nurses working in all types of surgical units need to understand the ways in which children and their families respond to a period of hospitalisation; how these effects can be ameliorated, and the principles of pre- and post-operative care which, together with the current research, rationale and evidence base underpins action. Doing this requires excellence in communication at all levels, the development of sound practical skills and the ability to evaluate performance through reflection in order to continually improve and refine care offered to children and their families.

References

Davis JL (1994) Perioperative care of the pediatric trauma patient *AORNJournal* **60**(4): 559, 561, 563–5

Department of Health (1991) *The Patient's Charter Raising the Standard*. HMSO, London

Edelstein J (1990) A study of nursing documentation *Nursing Management* **21**(11): 40-46

Field PA (1987) Doing fieldwork in your own culture. In: Morse J ed *Qualitative Nursing Research A Compemporary Dialogue*. Aspen Publishers, Tunbridge Wells

Fischbach FT (1991) *Documenting Care Communication, the Nursing Process and Documentation Standards*. FA Davies, Philadelphia

Gropper EI (1988) Does your chart reflect your worth? *Geriatric Nursing* March/April

Hunt JM, Marks-Maran DJ (1980) *Nursing Care Plans. The Nursing Process at Work*. John Wiley, Chichester

McKenna H (1990) Which model? Choosing a nursing model *Nursing Times* **86**(25): 50-2

Orem D (1985) *Nursing: Concepts of Practice* 3rd Edition. McGraw-Hill, New York

Roper N, Logan WW, Tierney AJ (1985) *The Elements of Nursing*. Churchill Livingstone, Edinburgh

Roy C (1976) *Introduction to Nursing. An Adaption Model*. Prentice-Hall, New Jersey

Smith F (1995) *Children's Nursing in Practice. The Nottingham Model*. Blackwell Science, Oxford

United Kingdom Central Council (1993) *Standards for Records and Record Keeping*. UKCC, London

Walton I (1986) Lessons from the Health Service Ombudsman's Reports. *Nursing Times* **82**(10): 54–7

Further reading

The texts below are accessible and informative on key issues and debates when considering the type of model to use and the ways in which these can inform practice.

Salvage J (1990) *Model for Nursing 2*. Scutari Press

Pearson A, Vaughan B (1986) *Nursing Models for Practice*. Butterworth-Heinemann, London

Walsh M (1991) *Models in Clinical Nursing the Way Forward*. Balliere Tindall, London

10

Discharge planning

Key issues and concepts

+ The purposes of discharge planning

+ Preparation for discharge

+ The impact of discharge on the family

+ Concepts of teaching and learning related to discharge

The purpose of discharge planning

Without doubt, nursing care planning for children during their admission is integral to the whole process of meeting assessed health care needs. Similarly, discharge planning is equally important and is also aimed at meeting health care needs, but the focus of such planning is directed towards enabling the child and their family to live with the consequences of surgery and ensuring that they have sufficient, appropriate information and teaching to be able to do so. Publication of *The Patient's Charter* (DoH, 1991) has prompted nurses to develop written information about surgery and follow-up care with the specific intention of meeting such needs. Although such leaflets are usually expertly produced, as a stand-alone technique of preparation for discharge they are insufficient and children's nurses need to think more globally about the issues surrounding discharge for children and their families. In order to achieve this, Brunner and Suddarth (1991) highlight a number of areas which are important to consider:

- detailed preparation for home care
- referral to appropriate community support services
- provision of resources to assist families to care for their child.

Detailed preparation for home care

Detailed preparation for home care is characterised by the attention that is paid to the specific information and special procedures that the child and/or their parents may need to perform once they have been discharged from hospital. Such information and procedural elements of discharge planning can include anything from discussion about the reasons for oral medication, to developing parent and child skill in temperature taking or more technical expertise such as maintaining the patency of intravenous access lines like Hickman catheters. Whatever the type of specific need, there are some common concepts related to both information giving and learning and teaching. Therefore, the children's nurse must be able to assess the nature of such needs, plan measures to meet the needs identified, and implement and evaluate the effectiveness of planned actions.

Assessing discharge needs

An assessment of discharge needs can and should be started at the time of the child's admission to hospital. This is feasible because it is often possible to predict specific needs especially where the type of surgery and its consequences is known. In addition, parents often have informational needs related to caring for their child when discharge is imminent and, where there is early preparation for discharge, the opportunity to ensure careful and individual planning and organisation to meet these needs exists. Therefore, at the assessment phase of discharge planning, the children's nurse must be able to identify what the family's discharge needs are likely to be, actual and potential; how these needs can best be met; when preparation will occur;

where it may need to take place, and who will be responsible for undertaking it.

Planning to meet identified discharge needs

Discharge preparation can be planned using a discharge checklist rather like the theatre checklist used in pre-operative care (see *Figure 10.1*) This checklist is useful in ensuring that all aspects of discharge have been attended to and that all preparations made for the child and family's discharge from hospital is documented. However, such a checklist should be used in conjunction with other methods of preparation, the most common methods of which are information-giving, in either verbal or leaflet format, and through the process of a learning and teaching interaction between parent/child and nurse. Certainly, neither of these processes are easy, and both have their pitfalls and limitations.

Figure 10.1: Discharge documentation (adapted from Smith, 1995)

Child's name: Surname: *Holden* First name: *Neil* Likes to be called: *Neil*	**Registration number:** *158973KB*	**Date of admission:** 4/11/97	**Consultant:** *Godfrey*
	Ward: *Penguin*	**Time:** *0800 hours*	**Child's nurse:** *Frances Marks* **Team:** *Duck*
Address: *4 Ashfield Bourton Fellenshire* **Telephone number:** *78102*	**Age:** *6yrs 6mths* **Date of birth:** *05:05:91* **Religion:** *Church of England*	**Reason for this admission:** *Removal of tonsils and adenoids*	**Reasons for previous admission:** *No previous admission* **Medical history of note:** *Recurrent sore throats over last 18mths requiring antibiotic therapy from GP*
Next of kin: *Nancy Holden* **Address:** *4 Ashfield Bournton Fellenshire* **Telephone Numbers** **Work:** *76706* **Home:** *78102* **Relationship to child:** *Mother*	**Social circumstances:** *Maternal grandparents are looking after Neil's siblings for the duration of admission. Will only visit if admission is longer than one night. Dad will visit after work. Mum has taken time off work to stay with Neil until he is ready to return to school*	**Child's understanding of reason for this admission:** *To make sore throat get better so he can go back to school*	**Will anyone be resident with the child:** Yes/No **Where:** *By Neil's bed* **Name:** *Nancy Holden*
Who does the child live with: *Mum, Dad and siblings* **Who has parental responsibility:** *Parents*	**Names and ages of brothers and sisters:** *Ffion aged 11yrs/Dean aged 8yrs*	**Parents' understanding of reason for admission:** *Removal of tonsils and adenoids*	**Medical diagnosis:** *Admitted for adenotonsillectomy*

Allergies: *None known*	**Parent facilities:** Fire regulations : *yes*	**Discharge checklist:** Parent(s)/child informed of planned discharge date: *YES 5.11.97*	**General practioner:** *Dr.Goldsmith* **Address:** *The Practice, High St, Bourton* **Telephone:** *79456*
Recent contact with any infectious diseases: *None known*	Ward contact number given *yes*	Parent(s)/child agree discharge appropriate: *YES*	**Health visitor Address:** *Not applicable*
Current medication: *None being taken*	Shower/toilet facilities: *yes* Parent's kitchen: *yes* Ward kitchen: *yes*	Discharge advice sheet given and explained: *GIVEN TO MUM* Necessary teaching completed: *INFECTION RECOGNITION* Equipment on loan: *NONE*	**Telephone:**
Height: *124cm* | **Weight:** *22kg*	Dining room facilities: *yes*	Outpatient appointment given: *BOOKED for 18.12.97* Medicines given: *NONE MUM HAS PARACETAMOL AT HOME* Own medicines returned: *N/A* GP letter given: *YES* Health visitor/other health care contacts informed *SCHOOL NURSE* Ward contact telephone number given: *YES* Discharge completed by: *H BELL* Date: *5.11.97*	**Other contacts (with names and address):** *School Nurse Mrs Dempsey The Practice, High St, Bourton*
Immunisation history: *All immunisations up to date to time of pre-school booster*	*All immunisations up to date to time of pre-school*		**Signature of nurse taken history:** *A.S.Glover* **Date:** *30/10/97*
Other information relevant to admission: *Neil and his mum attended pre-admission on 30th October 1997 (A.S.Glover 30/10/97) No other information gathered at admission to the ward. (F.J.Marks)*			**Signature of ward nurse:** *FJ Marks* **Date:** *4/11/97*

Information giving in this context has been widely discussed within children's nursing literature and from this there are clear findings which emerge (Macdonald, 1988; Bradford and Singer, 1991; Kanneh, 1991; Bailey and Caldwell, 1997). The standard of information-giving is good in that parents are often satisfied with the information they receive. However, there is evidence to suggest that parents would like more information about detailed matters concerning both the care and condition of their children whilst they are in hospital. In particular relation to discharge planning similar issues are raised. Bailey and Caldwell (1997) report that parents may need detailed and specific information about caring for their child at home for example, general care skills; what to do if their child became ill again; advice about medicines and information about outpatient appointments. Therefore, when planning the kind of information to give to parents on discharge it is important to ensure that such issues are accounted for as well as including aspects which are specific to the child's post-operative care.

It is also clear that parents receive information from a number of sources, some parts of which they may not be able to assimilate at all (Bradford and Singer, 1991; Bailey and Caldwell, 1997). Therefore, it is important to identify that information-giving related to discharge planning needs to be accurate, consistent and delivered in such a way that parents are able to interpret what they are told appropriately (Bradford and Singer, 1991). This may mean the development of systems to support information-giving with written materials such as leaflets and booklets which address the types of common questions asked about the particular procedure; what to look out for in the post-operative period; any special precautions which need to be taken, as well as issues surrounding return to usual levels of activity. However, with verbal and written forms of information giving, problems are commonly related to language difficulties, partly because of the terminology used to present relevant information or that the first language of the child and family is not English and in some cases that parents cannot read (Bailey and Caldwell, 1997). Therefore, children's nurses need to consider how to integrate information systems which take account of such issues, including the availability of an interpreter; leaflets and booklets printed in languages other than English; use of terms which are familiar to the family, or planning to implement the kinds of mechanisms which illiterate parents are used to using to remember important information, as part of their preparation of families for discharge.

Some parents will also need to learn how to undertake specific procedures, and planning for this kind of discharge preparation means that the children's nurse must think about the ways in which parents can best be helped to do this. However, it must also be acknowledged that some parents will not want or feel able to learn to adopt such a role in caring for their children and this is just as acceptable as meeting the needs of parents who want and feel able to do so.

The kinds of skills which parents learn prior to discharge are varied, but mainly correlate with the principles of procedures involved in, for example, wound dressings. This type of skill is referred to as a 'motor skill'. Learning motor skills requires practice because of the time it takes to produce a fluent, efficient movement throughout the stages involved in the particular procedure (Quinn, 1988; White and Ewan, 1991). Quinn (1988) cites Fitts and Posner (1967) when he suggests that in learning a skill there a three processes which occur as the skill is learned:

1. *The cognitive phase*, where the procedure for carrying out the skill is learned. The more complicated the procedure, the more lengthy the phase.

2. *The associative phase*, where the skill is carried out with beginning elements of a skilled performance.

3. *The autonomous phase*, where the skill is performed automatically and occurs with little thought about the next stage to be accomplished.

In facilitating this process there are a number of considerations which need to be made. Most importantly, the children's nurse needs to create an environment within which parents feel confident to learn. Kyriacou (1991) describes this environment as being relaxed, warm and psychologically supportive.

However, this is often difficult to achieve with the major difficulties surrounding ward based teaching being that parents and their children may be stressed by the admission itself; there may be a great deal of anxiety associated with learning the procedure; parents may worry about carrying out the procedure on their child, and the unforeseen consequences this might have. There may also be a limited amount of time in which parents can master such skills because of the proposed date of discharge which may add additional pressure when trying to learn the complexities of a new and unfamiliar skill. Therefore, it is essential that when planning to use such methods of discharge preparation, careful thought is given to the way in which such instruction will take place. It is also important to address how the procedure will be learned, for example, what types of equipment will be needed and where and on whom the initial practice will take place.

Implementing actions for discharge preparation

One of the easiest ways to begin implementing the teaching of a skill is to demonstrate it. However, White and Ewan (1991) suggest that if this is the chosen starting point for skills teaching, there are some important questions to ask about the underpinning reasons of using this method:

- what are the main points you want to make in the demonstration?
- is the relevance of the demonstration clear?
- have you provided opportunities for supervised practice?

Generally, the purpose of including a demonstration when teaching a skill is to allow the person watching to see what kind of performance they are aiming for in terms of speed and how the dressing, for example, should look once the procedure is complete (Quinn, 1988). It often helps to explain this to the parent, so that they do not become unduly worried that they should be able to achieve such a competent level of performance at their first attempt. During the demonstration, it is possible to highlight verbally, each step in the procedure, suggesting its relevance and value to the procedure as a whole so that when practice does occur, the parent can try to remember the reason why it should be attempted in a particular way. During practice attempts at new skills it is important that positive, constructive feedback is given (Quinn, 1988). This is so that confidence in carrying out the procedure can be encouraged, but at the same time inconsistencies and inaccuracies can be corrected. Of course, these are only some of the types of teaching methods that can be employed in practice, and as Ewles and Simnet (1985) highlight, there are a variety of teaching methods available to the practitioner that can be used depending upon the preference of the person being taught and the kind of instruction needed.

Evaluating discharge preparation

Evaluation of discharge planning and preparation can be evident in the way that parents are able to perform a particular skill prior to discharge from the ward. In other cases, evaluation can take place by asking parents questions about the information they have received to analyse whether understanding is accurate in pertinent areas. However, parameters of evaluation may not always be so obvious and feedback about the success of discharge planning and preparation may only be possible to judge in terms of the organisational aspects of the child and family's discharge, particularly where the child has had only a very short admission.

Referral to appropriate community support services

Increasingly, the impact of long-term hospitalisation on children is being recognised and this has resulted in discharge from hospital as soon as is practicable. In order to support early discharge even when the child has undergone major surgery, there has been a rise in the availability of children's nurses working in the community, often with specialist roles and with the specific intention of caring for children and their families in their own homes where possible. However, the number of specialist community children's nurses from area to area is variable (Audit Commission, 1986) Therefore, the implications for discharge planning and preparation are to ensure that where possible, appropriate referral is made to community children's nurses and in other areas where the service is not available, to relevant staff. This is to facilitate continual support by someone who is known to the family once they have left the security of the ward environment and to assist in the early assessment of the home situation so that appropriate planning can ensure the right services are in place prior to discharge with the result that complications are minimised (Brunner and Suddarth, 1991; Smith, 1995).

Provision of resources to assist families

To achieve the objective of shorter hospital admission and the provision of care for the child in their own home wherever possible, equipment loan is often a discharge issue. This is because recent technological advances have enabled parents to care for their child at home even when highly dependent care is required and can be supported by equipment which, until recently, would only have been seen in a ward setting. As well as the provision of physical resources to accomplish care at home, it is important to recognise that community children's nurses have a unique role in supporting the family in caring for their child at home. The kind of support which can be offered is not only in terms of carrying out skilled nursing procedures for the child, but is also in providing psychological support for families who may otherwise be isolated because of their child's condition (Smith, 1995). In addition, the children's community nurse also has a leading role in assisting families to care for their child on a practical basis, and in promoting the child's health through advice and teaching together with measures designed to help maintain normal growth and development of the child when surgery is complex, long-term or repeated. Therefore, where possible and appropriate, referral to these highly skilled members of the multidisciplinary team should be made as soon as discharge needs are recognised.

Summary

Discharge planning is just as important as any other aspect of care planning for a child and their family. Parents often feel great anxiety at taking their child home and away from the security of the ward environment. Indeed, some families will actually take on extra responsibility of their child's care upon discharge. Therefore, the nurses responsibility is to ensure that appropriate methods of discharge planning for the individual child and family have been delivered to facilitate physical and psychological safety of the whole family once they return home. In co-ordinating discharge planning, the children's nurse has a central role, making decisions to refer children to appropriate services and instigating channels of liaison, so that family needs continue to be met throughout the period following discharge.

References

Audit Commission (1986) *Making a Reality of Community Care: A Report.* HMSO, London

Bailey R, Caldwell C (1997) Preparing parents for going home *Paediatr Nurs* **9**(4): 15–17

Bradford R, Singer H (1991) Suport and information for parents *Paediatr Nurs* **3**(4): 18–20

Brunner LS, Suddarth DS (1991) *The Lippincott Manual of Paediatric Nursing* 3rd Edition. Chapman and Hall, London

Department of Health (1991) *The Patient's Charter.* HMSO, London

Ewles L, Simnet I (1985) *Promoting Health: A Practical Guide to Health Education.* John Wiley, New York

Kanneh A (1991) Communicationg with care. *Paediatr Nurs* **3**(3): 24–27

Kyriacou C (1991) *Essential Teaching Skills*. Blackwell Education, London

Macdonald M (1988) Children discharged from hospital—what mothers want to know. *Nursing Times* **84**(16): 63

Quinn FM (1988) *The Principles and Practice of Nursing Education* 2nd Edition. Chapman and Hall, London

Smith F (1995) *Children's Nursing in Practice. The Nottingham Model*. Blackwell Science, Oxford

White R, Ewan C (1991) *Clinical Teaching in Nursing*. Chapman and Hall, London

Index

A
abnormalities 98
accurate recording 74
active drainage systems 64
admission 2, 13
airway 91
   - airway obstruction 40
anaesthesia 1
anaesthetic 1
analgesia 54, 88
anger 104
apical pulse rate 43
aspiration 41
assessment 17, 25, 36, 80
   - discharge needs 139
   -initial 26
   - in-depth
   - pain 58
   - thorough and accurate 25

B
baseline
   - information 25
   - observations 30
behaviour 119
   - of the child 46
   - likely 94
bereavement 101
blood pressure 25, 42, 44
   - pressure regulation 45
bonding and attachment
  processes 77
Bowlby 4
breathing 91
   - patterns 25

C
case history 112
characteristics 102
child's contribution 17
children's casualty departments 91
circulation 91
circulatory status 42
Clothier Report 100
collaboration 24
community children's nurses 147
community staff 80

complications 39
concept of illness 4
concerns of children and their
  families 93
concrete operational stage 4
congenital abnormality 73
consent 30 ,34
   - to surgery 18
   - informed 35
conserve 5
consistency in caring 95
constructive feedback 146
contagious anxiety 17
contamination 46
co-ordinating 24
coping mechanism 58, 94
Court Report 83
cultural and religious beliefs 101

D
day case surgery 3, 85
   - advantages and disadvantages
   84
death of a child 98
dehiscence 67
dehydration 33
delivery of nursing care 25
developmental ability 26
diastolic 44
discharge 36
   - planning 138
documentation 32
   - effective 109

E
elective surgery 10, 23
electrolyte
   - balance 74
   - imbalance 33
emergency 23
   - situation 54
   - treatment 35
emotional
   - costs of hospitalisation 83
   - responses 102
ensorimotor stage 4
enteral feeds 75